AMERICAN AUTOMOBILES

OF THE 50s AND 60s

ALBERTO MARTINEZ
JEAN-LOUP NORY

Motorbooks International
Publishers & Wholesalers Inc
Osceola, Wisconsin 54020, USA ®

Copyright 1986 by Motorbooks International.
ISBN: 0-87938-226-0

Motorbooks International is a certified trademark, registered
with the United States Patent Office.
Printed and bound in France.

Motorbooks International books are also available at discounts in
bulk quantity for industrial or sales-promotion use.
For details write to Marketing Manager, Motorbooks International,
P.O. Box 2, Osceola, Wisconsin 54020.

contents

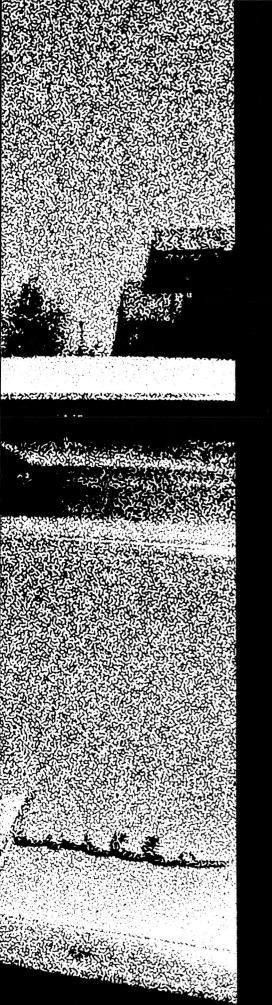

Flavour
of the Fifties

We've been driving for hours through the pitch black night of the Nevada desert; it's nearly four in the morning and day is breaking, and a kind of huge joy is welling up inside me. Tiredness recedes and the muddy thoughts that have been churning in my head by the light of the instrument panel disappear.

I still can't see much. A thin strip of light hovers on the horizon, still crushed between the dark blue of heaven and earth. In fact everything is dark blue, but you know that will change soon. That once again the long straight line we're rolling on, straighter than a builder's plumb line, will reappear out front of our long hoods.

Two cars — alone — on this Interstate highway. A 57 Ford Fairlane Skyliner, followed by a white Cadillac convertible with red leather upholstery. Two specimens rarely seen nowadays, two monsters dripping chrome and laden with horsepower that would leave today's automotive efforts standing. Especially the Caddy. Nearly 345 horsepower superbly served by a four-speed automatic box that gets you to 100 mph in third and rockets you to 125 mph a few seconds later.

A thoroughbred set of wheels!

Not a cop in sight, just the two V8s running in perfect condition. One hour from now we'll be crossing Las Vegas, soon after we'll be at Lake Tahoe on the Californian frontier for a Fifties' meet. It was last night that we spotted the two Fifties' cars parked close to a Burger King. We exchanged a few words of car-talk. Since we were all going in the same direction to the same spot, it was a matter of course that we should drive there together.

So here we are. All that remains for me to do is to talk about the cars, the times and motoring phenomena that have gone forever but that left such a mark on their quarter-century that you all know what it was about. Only — the whys and wherefores of chrome and fins, the infatuation with eighteen-foot monsters coloured pale pink or emerald green; these are things that defy reason, logic. So my aim will be to present these facts and fancies in such a way that every mind whatever its capacity, can read these lines without losing the thread.

When the end of World War II arrived, the Americans, without whose aid we would still be in a hole, returned to their "home sweet home". Their joy was understandable, but their industrial machine was greatly damaged. The economy was barely ticking over and factories did their best to resume activities but were interrupted by strikes and plunged into a dearth of raw materials. Against this scenario the car had a tough time surviving, for two reasons: first, the lack of time needed to create new models, second, the scarceness and high price of steel. Thus it was that the famous marque of Packard, then beating Cadillac in the sales war, fell behind to second place in 1949 for failing to purchase sufficient metal at the high prices (a decision taken by its incompetent president, nicknamed "Pinchpenny" who was duly put out to grass on his Texas ranch to meditate upon his folly).

Up to 1947, in fact, the three major motor manufacturers as well as the small ones were content just to continue with the pre-war models: split windscreens, prominant hoods with distinctly separate fenders, and unexciting side-valve straight six or straight eight engines.

Do you know what was the first real novelty after the war, in styling I mean? Listen well, you may not like it: it was the Studebaker. That's right, the "Stude" as designed by the brilliant Frenchborn, Raymond Loewy. Front fenders were integrated into the engine compartment (unit construction) and the grille was now horizontal (no longer vertical). So violent was this new car (the Starlight) that unkind voices (of which there were not a few) asked how to tell the front from the back. Most critics could not take the radical change, so accustomed were they to their pre-war wrecks! Narrow minds burst blood vessels, far preferring (in 1947) the outdated shapes of Ford or even of General Motors who naturally got first prize for sales: 1,430,00 units sold by GM, 770,000 for Ford, while the "Stude" was sold out at 123,000 copies.

Then there was the second revolution in style, the one that truly heralded the Fifties. This was the "new American automobile culture". I feel obliged at this point to go a little deeper into detail since this was a style and way of life never seen in Europe. It's worth dragging our feet around the corridors of Cleveland or Detroit, not far, just a few miles.

This second revolution therefore was the fin. The fin phenomenon is a story all of its own, and goes something like this: the chief designer of GM was a nice guy named Harley Earl who stood well over six-foot-four. One day he stopped right in front of a Lockheed P.38 fighter aircraft, a three-fuselage combat plane, with two of its fuselages ending in a graceful fin. The idea occurred to him to use these excrescences on cars. And so it was that "prefins" appeared on the 1947 Cadillac to become veritable protruberances in 1948. The fins grew and grew, going hand-in-hand with bullet — or "Dagmar" — bumpers, finally going over the top with shattering and aggressive folly during 58, 59 and 60. These meagre words on styling are intended to show that the manufacturers essential objective was to innovate at all costs and to astonish the public. Commonsense cars went out the window. Besides, once the first few years of the Fifties were over, steel became plentiful and the American motorist was witness to the most incredible orgy of chrome as both a symbol of power and a reflection of traditional aesthetics. Armoured like a tank, the car became a mirror reflecting the soul of its owner, a thing of power and seduction. As the years passed, production burgeoned like a chicken fed on hormones. In 1949 GM turned out 2,200,000 cars, Chrysler made 1,120,000 and Ford 1,020,000, while

the little-big manufacturers varied between 230,000 and 60,000 (Studebaker and Kaiser-Frazer respectively).

But enough of boring statistics, let them suffice to give an impression of the revival of the American automobile industry after the war. It was a revival which brought with it socio-economic and material consequences felt by American citizens in terms of a thirst for refrigerators, air conditioning and long, low cars.

Thanks to the huge range of models available, practically every American family owned at least one car before 1950. Things got so that all of American life revolved around the car. There was no getting away from it: freeways pushed out in all directions, cutting the time spent behind the big steering wheel. The cities themselves were built to cater for the car. There were huge parking lots so you could park right in front of the store door, while the suburbs became places of residence with space enough to have a double garage; down town was kept mainly for business.

Yes indeed, a different lifestyle was rapidly descending on the Americans. Without a car, Man became a wild beast lost inside cities that stretched out for dozens of miles in all directions. The car became Man's second nature. And Woman's. She could go to the bank, the laundromat and even the restaurant without even so much as getting out of the car. Imagine the revolution! A lifestyle that the French cannot begin to guess at with their curious "Quatre Chevaux", their "traction à vent" and that famous Vedette designed in 1947 by Ford America only to be consigned to the trash can and then resurrected again — thanks for nothing!

It was an age when people seemed to live by the motto; "A car, a job, a girl, a house", and in that order! For the kids at least, you couldn't get a girl without a car. So if Dad was in a good mood and didn't spill his hamburger sauce over his shirt sleeve, he'd lend you his car for the

evening, and life was transformed totally.

Then you'd go to the drive-in or the snack bar and spend your time dancing and buying hand-made hamburgers. At the time, this food was super and American teenagers consumed it incessantly, something which they are still doing today, so it seems.

And if you lived in a small village without a freeway link, it was often an expedition with six or eight of you in search of those places of perdition.

The drive-in movie was one of the inner sanctums of American youth. The open-air cinema was what they went for, but not many of these nice kids were worried about what was happening on screen. They had their hands full with the sweet little chick sitting right next to them, or perhaps not so close depending on the mood of the moment.

There was even a car specially designed for the drive-in, the Nash Airflyte (1949) nicknamed "the Bathtub". This car, whose particularly aerodynamic styling left one with the impression of a huge slug; had a rather intimate feel about it. And there was more. The front seat squabs reclined to form a couchette — see what I'm getting at? Before you can say "two-lane blacktop" the kid has pushed a lever and his ingenuous girlfriend is on her back, not

an easy position to watch the film from. The Airflyte, whose interior resembled nothing so much as a submarine, quickly got a lot of bad press among puritanical families who saw in it a terrible place of perdition. Fathers who owned the car suddenly stopped lending it to their sons, while the girl's parents forbade her to even look at it.

The long evenings were spent happily listening to the throb of the big V8 or straight six just ticking over. There wasn't much to do in a small provincial town, so the kids just cruised around at 10 mph in search of female company while listening to the car's valve radio.

The "underground auto culture" in fact started sometime around 1948, crystallizing around the drive-in, the most famous of which was the Piccadilly close to Sepulveda Boulevard (Los Angeles). There were roadsters, Forties' type B8 40 three-window Ford Coupes, custom cars and a whole range of rods. Each day Sepulveda Boulevard featured "cruisin's", a kind of slow, stately procession, bumper-to-bumper. Often there would be hundreds of kids just watching the monster cars drive by, sitting on the fender of their cars parked on the sidewalk. It was at this time that the myth of the 400 metre standing start, or quarter mile, was born, i.e. the distance from one

Fewer than 2000 1957 Mercury Turnpike Cruiser convertibles were made. It was pace car at the Indianapolis 500

block to the next, or even better, the distance between two lights. Towards midnight or in the wee small hours the kids would line up in pairs, then the light switched to green and.... hammer down. The two cars rear up on their back suspension. Tyres burn rubber for an instant, and the first one to the next light wins. Later on, Sepulveda Boulevard was abandoned in favour of Compton where the races were held on the highway. It was safer! With the cars starting on either side of the central reservation, there was no risk of a tangle. At Compton they held real races at the crack of dawn; the kids who were there to watch parked each side of the highway and lit up the track with their headlights. The highway was blocked at each end, and provided the cops stayed away the races were real duels to the death fought by super-hyped engines.

And so young America discovered a passion for engines and for speed, a passion tragically culminating several years later in the death of James Dean, killed at the wheel of his Porsche Speedster near Salinas between Los Angeles and San Francisco.

It has to be said that motor manufacturers very quickly took up the challenge of power, and technology progressed at a devil's pace while each marque tried everything to outdo and supplant its immediate rival. From 1948 on, the Cadillac was fitted with a high-compression V8, followed by pneumatic suspension long before today's hydraulic systems; then came fully automatic transmissions, the most incredible electrical systems, and a photoelectric cell that switched high beam to low automatically. Little by little, cars equipped with power brakes and steering, and if you are of a mind to pursue the matter further, you will find that the Americans were a lot less ignorant on these things than we think they were. At least in matters of the automobile during that great period of the Fifties. They were in fact in the process of inventing motoring monsters with the aim, first to perpetuate the great tradition of splendid pre-war American cars, and second, to establish the myth of the long, super-powered limousine gliding silently and effortlessly over the new interstates. Something to bring joy to the hearts of teenagers still dreaming of English cars and speed.

Today, nothing has gone. The Fifties are returning with a vengeance, and with them, the cars, They are coming out of garages, emerging from junk yards. Wtih patient and loving restoration they are becoming part of America's automobile heritage, thanks to the nostalgia of the old kids and their parents.

1958 was marked by swathes of chrome encasing the cars, especially their rear fenders like on this Buick Century. Next page *An Oldsmobile 98 Starfire convertible of 1955 — note the symmetrical design of the dashboard and the handle next to the steering wheel to control the exterior searchlight*

CHRYSLER CORPORATION

This incredible Chrysler
Town and Country of
1948 is powered by a 135
hp straight eight. The
timber members are in
ash, giving high
dimensional stability! Left
of the loudspeaker, the
radio changed colour
when a new station was
selected

Chrysler

Chrysler

There are times, dear reader, when the joy of driving does not lie in the science of the side-slip, when last-chance braking and taking corners on three wheels becomes heresy, like maple syrup on a shirt collar. In Europe, of course, we cannot imagine a car without knowing its top speed and performance data. But there are other times, gentle, sensual moments, which can easily send you into a state of bliss. I know you will laugh when I confess that I had a lot of fun driving a Chrysler Town and Country around in a sedate fashion, with its overblown dashboard detail, twiddling the giant-size radio knobs while I polished the horn ring with my shirt sleeve. And why not, when half of it is made of wood, like the 1946 Town and Country. And when I admit that I enjoyed driving this comfortable sloth, you will die laughing.

That, basically, is what postwar de luxe automobiles were all about. No brilliant engines, just a finish and trim to stop you dead in your tracks. Like that aggressive red Chrysler with its heavy grille and madly elaborate timber rear end — yes, real timber! A lot went into that finish, a creation by specialist craftsmen and painstaking detail that made this convertible the most celebrated drophead of its day. It was well worth its 2743 dollars, a reasonable price considering the work that went into that wood. They used ash for the main members because of its dimensional stability, while the in-fill panels were lined with a sheet of mahogany that was replaced in 1947 by imitation wood decals — what a come-down! But it was not only the making of the car that was a whole work of art — and a very expensive one at that: its upkeep and maintenance cost a fortune too. 298 dollars just to replace a quarter panel, while on the standard convertible the bill came to just 66 dollars! Which was why Chrysler were unable to offer its customers this magnificent luxury and rustic beauty for very long. This whole business was not exactly profitable Nevertheless, the marque could take pride in the knowledge that it had created a veritable jewel whose merits were not restricted to its timbers. There was the radio. A valve radio, of course, and of a devilish sophistication, with its tuning strip changing colour as the volume increased. Next to the speaker, the clock, above it the two-speed wiper switch — the wipers were electrically operated, not vacuum. Dual heating system, ventilation at all levels and never an ounce of mist. Its speedometer, marked off up to 110 miles per hour, changed colour as the speed increased: green up to 30, orange up to 50, then red. Not to mention its cigar lighter, the two exterior rear-view mirrors, the parking-brake warning light (intermittent!), electric hood and choice of eight body colours. What have we got that can compare? Nothing but the sole choice of our resentment.

In 1946 Chrysler still believed in the virtues and resources of the in-line engine. Cadillac started to make V8s in 1915, while Ford introduced them in the early Thirties. A refinement not to be found on the Town and Country. Instead, it had a hefty in-line eight, all in cast iron, block and head. The crankshaft had five journal bearings, and the whole engine was based on the original 1934 design. With a capacity of 323 cu.in. and a compression ratio of 6.8:1, this beast developed its 135 horsepower at 3400 rpm with torque of 270 foot-pounds at 1000 rpm. The carburettor was a Carter, lubrication was pressurized.

The engine's oil capacity was 6 litres, the cooling system's 27.

After all this, the aluminium pistons were rather daring. The other mechanical features were taken from the Chrysler New Yorker, and somewhat ordinary at that: rear axle with

Panhard rod on leaf springs, worm and peg steering, hydraulic drum brakes. The car's originality, if it can be called that, was its gearbox. Many cars were already fitted with fully automatic transmissions, like GM for instance. But the Chrysler people were reluctant to launch themselves into this unknown, and preferred to design a semi-automatic, since despite its Fluid-Drive hydraulic coupler, the box had a normal clutch. In fact, first and third gears were manual in the classic mode, while second and fourth were automatic. Not till 1953 was the entire Chrysler range fitted with the fully automatic two-speed Powerflite transmission.

So was the Town and Country a success? Aesthetically, yes. With its two tons elegantly distributed over a length of 17.85 feet, it gave an impression of power and ostentation that we find later in 1955 on the 300. Unfortunately, this gentleman's automobile was expensive and took a long time to build. Only 1936 convertibles were made in 1946, 3137 in 1947 and 2936 in 1948; production came to halt completely in the second month of 1949 (374 cars).

The 1948 Coupe Royal, magnificently shown in the pages of this de luxe book on cars of tradition, was to become the darling of hot-rod lovers (or drivers of "street machines" as they were called up to 1948). To the hot-rodder, this was the "three window coupe" and when you had fitted it with a 300 or 400 hp V8 and Jaguar rear axle, it became one of the greats in the history of American custom cars. But that did not happen to this superb example, a perfect original, with but 37,000 miles on the clock, its brilliant paintwork and mechanics are fit to do Miami - Los Angeles on two wheels.

The name of this coupe was deceptive. In fact it was called the Business Coupe (or Three Passengers Coupe), thus clearly indicating its down-to-earth utility despite its masculine assurance and irreprochable elegance. Behind the bench seat we find a lot of space for luggage, which is why it had only three windows. The same coupe, but with five windows, was called the "Club Coupe" and had two bench seats. If the word "Club" does lend an air of luxury to the vehicle, I still prefer the Business Coupe with its nonchalant, sprawling look, first because its appearance is perfect, dominated

A 1947 Chrysler Royal, named the "Business Coupe", featured a single bench seat and "three windows"

Chrysler

1956 four-door Chrysler
New Yorker with definite
fin formation

Chrysler

Panoramic windshield and a restrained grille. The coachwork is well set off by the two-tone colour scheme

Chrysler

The famous Chrysler "300" appeared in 1955 with its 300 horsepower; above, the 300-F of 1960 with deck showing outside spare effect

mainly as it is by the outsize (and often totally useless) boot. The grille may be the same as on the Town and Country, but the rest of the body is more confident and sober.

It's all a matter of taste, as they say. And they are right.

But that does not stop me liking this little monster — current asking price in the States: 5000-6000 dollars. It had an in-line six cylinder engine of 4 litres capacity developing 112 horsepower. Transmission was the Fluid Drive, and the rest of the chassis was the same as the Windsor, which meant conventionality fringing on the trite, except for the "independent" front wheels.

Do you know what the great mechanical revolution was at Chrysler was during the Fifties? Obviously not. It was the introduction in 1951 of the first V8 of the marque, the Fire Power. Why revolutionary?

There were several reasons. The first was its modern design, with hemispherical combustion chambers and high compression ratio (7.5:1). Second, it was the most powerful V8 around at the time: 180 hp at 4000 rpm compared with 160 for the Cadillac of the same size: 331 cubic inches. And finally, because it had been on the drawing board ever since 1937, which meant that the end

result was perfect — we hope. But in 1953, two years later, Chrysler's 180 hp were overtaken by Cadillac's 210, a temporary setback that did not bother Chrysler.

In 1955, thanks to a new cam design, a four-barrel carburettor and twin exhausts, the rating was stepped up to 250 hp from the same 331 cubic inches. The engine was fitted to the up-range models, the New Yorker and the Imperial.

The four-door sedan shown here is a 1956 New Yorker, coded C-72.

Unlike the Cadillac, its lines were almost entirely free from nauseating ornaments. Discreet fins starting from halfway down the body and relatively massive bumpers did not alter its simple contours. As for the mechanics, the engine had grown yet again, with a capacity increased to 354 cubic inches and a rating of 280 horsepower.

Behind it, the Power Flite auto transmission. Power brakes and steering, electric windows, not to mention the incredible heating/ventilation system that worked on petrol and that generated a temperature of 100 degrees Fahrenheit in a matter of seconds! Another innovation was its push-button gear selection — no longer the column shift — a feature that became a Chrysler tradition. Despite its air of a heavy, cumbersome sedan, the New Yorker possessed first-class driving manners. Its steering was gentle and precise, its brakes nonfade and long-lasting. The most impressive aspect was its performance coupled with its excellent roadholding. Its top speed approached 110 mph without effort and with perfect handling. 0 to 60 in 10.5 seconds, no mean feat for the period and the car's two tons of weight. All in all a sporty sedan, but way behind the fabulous Chrysler 300-C of 1955.

The 300-C, labelled as "fantastic" by the press of the time, was the work of a certain Robert McGregor, Chrysler's chief engineer. The model shown here is the 300-F coupe of 1960, and though the car's styling might have changed, its sporty soul remained.

Chrysler

In August 1954, Chrysler management decided to build a competition car whose styling would as far as possible resemble series-produced vehicles. At the beginning, Virgil Exner, the stylist, decided to borrow the New Yorker's body modified with some parts from the Imperial, like the grille. The engine was still the basic 331 cubic inches. The whole idea was to increase output to 300 horsepower, and to do this they adapted the special camshaft as used on the 1954 Le Mans Cunningham. Carburation was provided by dual four-barrels. And so that the car's roadholding could take the huge increase in power, the suspension was lowered and stiffened. Then the finished article was taken to Daytona for a series of test runs to prove its sporty pretensions. 0 to 60 was covered in 9.8 seconds, 0-90 in 16.9, while top speed, wait for it, was recorded at 130 miles per hour. All this thanks to the good services of the Power Flite transmission. To finish with, and to make everybody happy, the car was put on the market with four different rear axle ratios. The basic price was 4055 dollars, nearly 500 more than the New Yorker. The optional radio, heating and power steering cost an extra 300 dollars.

Chrysler's directors immediately entered the C-300 in NASCAR races which it won one after the other. It was a total success that the old stagers of the time, Nash, Hudson et al, were unable to beat.

This incredible automobile, a car to send shivers down the spine of any teenager capable of comprehending the motion of a piston, this power-laden machine, did not stop in 1955 but went from strength to strength in successive years. In 1956 it became the 300-B logically enough. This time around, capacity was up at 3543 cubic inches and the rating at 340 hp; compression ratio was 9:1. And there's more to come, in the shape of an option putting the compression 10:1 and output at 355 hp. 0 to 60 mph fell to 8.4 seconds and top speed rose to 139 miles per hour.

Options still included half a dozen different differentials from 3.08 to 6.17, the latter giving a 0-60 time of an incredible 4 seconds!

1957 brought a fresh body-blow for the competitors of the C-300, the Big-C: an entirely new line with a very pure styling, majestic fins slowly rising skyward and an aggressive grille. The 300 was available as a coupe or convertible. Its engine capacity now stood at 392 cubic inches giving a standard rating of 375 hp with an optional 390! Some added refinements helped the owner to keep a grip on all that power: more accurate steering, a fan that could be cut out at 2500 revs, plus stiffer torsion bars. With all that fire in its belly, this terrifying motor car now had a maximum speed of 150 mph.

Come 1958, a new year and a new car, the 300-D (LC3-S), almost devoid of any alteration to styling with the exception of a simplified grille. It was just as beautiful, monstrous and incredibly fast, with the same engine and the same output. The innovation was fuel injection which we find elsewhere on the Corvette. But sad to say, the injection system had not been perfected and the anticipated 390 hp never materialized. The injection system — called Electrojector — was poison: the first sixteen cars fitted with it had to be converted back to twin carbs and to 375 horsepower.

In 1960 the 300 series had an "F" added, with the same power.

But it's hardly worth reciting a string of technical details that have no basic interest. Suffice it to say that the 300 series continued on into the Seventies without ever again attaining the heights of virility and technical virtuosity achieved in the Fifties.

We can state quite honestly that the most powerful of the series-manufactured Chryslers died at the beginning of the Sixties, and that the greatest year of the 300 will always be its first — 1955.

Chrysler

New Yorker wagon of 1955 with fins poorly integrated into the vehicle's main styling. Clock was mounted in the centre of the steering wheel; at left, the pushbutton auto controls. Opposite, *the knife-blade contours of the 300-F*

Chrysler

De Soto

Who remembers the DeSoto marque? Does the name mean anything to you? A name of Latin origins, centuries old, and borrowed from a Spanish conquistador. When you put the question, the answers are evasive, patchy, or just plain wrong. In fact, this all-American marque never made it big in Europe, and besides, it disappeared way back in 1961. Created in 1928 by Walter Chrysler to fill the gap between his Dodges and Plymouths, the DeSoto's success was quick to come. They were simple cars, simple to the point of primitive, but at the same time robust, and the public of the day immediately recognized a safe, value-for-money product.

Thus it was that the DeSoto built up a reputation as a medium range car possessing road characteristics and a reliability that were indisputable.

The model brought out straight after the war (1945) was a big sedan whose front end had been on the drawing boards for years. The story goes that Buzz Grisinger, the marque's chief designer and stylist, had designed a dreamcar project during the war whose novel styling was based on very attractive curves, a rounded roof with equally rounded integral windows, plus a fine grille in the shape of teeth. The headlamps were fully integrated in the fenders just like the pre-war Cords.

Sadly, this project was shelved but the sedan that was brought out in 1942 took up the idea of the teeth grille and the integral headlamps. Despite its large production numbers this car has become extremely rare today, even in the States.

Immediatly after the war a similar car rolled off the production lines, having lost the battle of the disappearing headlamps, which had proved too costly to make. The years 1946 to 1949 saw the production of a popular sedan endowed with an essential quality: toughness.

This car was the DeSoto S II Custom with styling characterized by a heavy unit body with large-surface panels, just like in the Thirties, and small window areas. But the best of all was the grille, a monstrous structure with cat's teeth that looked alive but weren't, thank God. An outstanding feature that cried out for love, respect and plenty of polish every day. A closer look at the S II reveals non-integral fenders that look really good. Bumpers followed the current fashion and were stronger than a prison door. On the subject of doors, these opened unusually to the rear to facilitate access and egress by the occupants. One most notable fact was that, apart from the grille, the car was devoid of chrome and there was no hint of those provocative fins that sealed the fate of the DeSoto marque fifteen years later.

Under the hood we come face to face with the banality and coldness of cast-iron. The engine block with side valves had a total capacity of 237 cu.in., with six cylinders giving a respectable 109 hp at 3600 rpm. Not much admittedly, but we must not forget that the Americans of the day, especially the middle-class American housewife, were unaware of electric gadgets, at least in this class of car, and that the overall weight was not excessive: 3740 lb. Maximum torque was 22.4 mkg and the compression ratio never bettered 6.6 : 1. The carburettor was a simple Carter unit, while cooling was handled by 16 litres of liquid. Which means that in today's traffic holdups the beast would never warm up at all.

Transmission was not all that simple because out of the four forward gears, two were manual and two automatic — this was the famous Fluid Drive so dear to the hearts of Chrysler. This was in actual fact a semi-automatic box with hydro-electric control, but the clutch was standard hydraulic. This part of the mechanics was the most sophisticated of the entire car, the rest of the

De Soto

chassis comprising four hydraulic drum brakes that were not power assisted, coil spring suspension at front and a rigid rear axle on semi-elliptics. Inside, the sole piece of daring was the dashboard. While less elaborate and less dazzling than the up-market Chryslers, it neverless retained the essential flavour of luxury. It was extremely comprehensive, with the main dial incorporating the speedometer, fuel gauge, water temperature, oil pressure and amps. As one expected, the speedo needle changed colour as speed increased. The radio was a masterpiece. Fully chrome-plated from top to bottom, it featured preselect buttons with a colour band that changed according to the programme. Not bad for a car of its class. In terms of performance, the engine — a design nearer to the Forties than the Fifties — provided satisfactory service. Top speed was around 95 mph and was, one has to admit, attained fairly quickly.

The relatively heavy weight of the body did not compromise acceleration and enabled the car to maintain good average performances. While the steering was very high-ratio, it was at least smooth and precise, something which the DeSoto of the Fifties were gradually to lose. Only the brakes come in for real criticism today. They required frequent adjust-

ment and their efficiency left a lot to be desired. In the same years the S II Custom's companion model was the Suburban limousine, a car that was more suited to the duties of a taxi rather than as a large family hold-all. At the beginning of the Fifties the entire Chrysler Corporation overtook Ford on sales, chiefly due to its mid-range, middle-of-the-road models like the DeSoto and the Dodge, neither of them particularly attractive vehicles in themselves. Even in their Sportsman and De Luxe versions, they continued to live with the old six-cylinder whose power never ever reached 120 hp. Not till 1952 did a new model appear, the Firedome with its small V8 of 276 cubic inches putting out 160 horsepower at 4000 rpm, and power brakes. The year after, the whole range was restyled, with that famous teeth grille. The facelift was accompanied by new names like Powermaster and Powerflite. The V8 upgraded by 10 hp and overdrive was optional.

In the midst of all this mechanical action which, though not extensive was nevertheless logical given the Corporation's reluctance to revamp their models every single year, we can see that the external facelift was not exactly startling. There were innovations, of course, but the new

DeSoto

1947 DeSoto Sedan
showing off its majestic
and comprehensive
dashboard. It's straight
six permitted a good 90
mph top speed. The rear
doors were rear-hung to
facilitate passenger access.
Opposite *The "rainfall"
grille and "Fluid Drive"
motif — this was a kind
of semi-automatic
transmission*

DeSoto

"Teeth" grille of the 1954 DeSoto, powered by a 170 hp V8

fashion of fins passed DeSoto by totally.

In 1955 the range was again restyled, and this time the rear fenders did reveal some small excrescences, hardly worth a mention at all, in fact, were it not that the following year, 1956, they exploded into full view.

The body was once more restyled, and to such a degree that DeSotos which hitherto had looked pretty puny suddenly seemed by comparison monumental and imposing by virtue of their gigantic fins that ended in a point and three protruding tail lights. Existing names like Firedome (230 horsepower at 4400 rpm) and Fireflite, an intermediate model with 255 hp at 4400 rpm, were reinforced by the new Adventurer Coupe.

So what was the reason for this sudden and brutal novelty? The Adventurer had nothing at all to do with the other models in the range. It featured a big 341 cubic inch V8 developing 320 hp at 5200 rpm. This was the main event within the DeSoto marque, a complete turnround in an old-established image. To regild their rather tarnished shield, the DeSoto bosses wanted an aggressive and powerful car that could measure up to the new Chrys-

ler C-300 whose potential we have already seen. In 1956 DeSoto was looking like a real conqueror, gone was that hangdog look of tired models propelled by tired engines. This time with its 320 horsepower it was the fastest after the Chrysler 300-B, of course, which in that same year offered an optional 340 or 350 hp engine. DeSoto had made the breakthrough and were Pace Car at Indianapolis to prove it. But it was just the Adventurer with its 320-odd horsepower which enabled the marque to boost its sales. This low-production car with all its prestige was required to carry models that were less glamorous but more economical. In 1957 it was decided to bring out a new basic model, the Firesweep, with the same body for the top-of-the-range cars, the Firedome and Fireflite. The prestige models were given twin headlamps, a feature that spread to all models by 1958 with the exception of batches of cars shipped to certain States that were still rejecting this novelty. Still in 1957, DeSoto, now 29 years old as a marque, took a fresh look at its engines and proposed three new V8's with 325, 341 and 345 cubic inch capacities; ratings ranged from 245 to 345 horsepower, the latter being reserved for the Adventurer Coupe.

De Soto

In the middle of this veritable plethora of new models, engines, optional extras and bodies facelifted each year, the American automobile was beginning to flag. In 1958 all motor manufacturers were affected by sales that were dropping in free fall. The major manufacturers were able to weather the storm, but DeSoto, financially isolated from Chrysler Corporation, were unable to invest to expand their network and rethink their cars.

The 1958 reflects this basic weakness: there were no changes, a fact that put off a major block of DeSoto customers. A few minor details were revamped, like bumpers and side mouldings, but it just was not enough. 1958, the year that the factory celebrated its Thirtieth birthday and looked back on a prosperous past, marked the beginning of the end. Total sales fell by 55,000 units over 1957 despite the sixteen different models on offer. Despite the still powerful V8s and the Adventurer which by now boasted 355 plus under its hood.

The following year only confirmed the slow but inevitable downhill slide. Without any resources to invest, the monstrous DeSotos of 1956 with their rear-jutting fins and tail lights pointed like lighthouses were merely the shadow of their former selves. The styling department did its best, but the funds were just not there. The general lines remained, and the public got bored.

1960 saw a last-ditch effort before the final catastrophe, the closure of the factory and with it the disappearance of a famous Spanish name. The panels were entirely restyled but with a marked lack of taste and an outdated look: massive grilles like wrought-iron palace gates, fins that sprouted from the centre of the front doors. Having lost its prestige and the confidence of its customers, DeSoto disappeared without trace at the dawn of the Sixties, just 33 years after its first factory had opened its doors.

Of all this noble history there are two things worth remembering, two cars. Buzz Grisinger's Dream Car that was to be the forerunner of all the models from 42 to 48. And the Adventurer, that terrifying, demon vehicle that could blast from 0 to 60 mph in 8 seconds but which, having got up to 110 just lost its legs.

The very last DeSoto featured those really bizarre fins, nicknamed "shark's nose" — perhaps an unconscious sign of the submergence of the marque into the depths of oblivion.

DeSoto Fireflite sedan of 1955 with engine rated at 200 hp while the Firedome had under 185 hp. Next page A 1959 pillarless four-door Firedome Sportsman, showing off its "rocket-launcher" taillights

Dodge

Dodge — now there's a name that sounds good! That conjures up the smell of the West and the dust of the wide-open spaces. The Dodge brothers, John and Horace, lived around the good old days of the 1900s. Sensing that the hour of the automobile was imminent, they began to build engines, gearboxes and rear axles, finally creating their own car, a modest little thing with four cylinders. But history relates that they came to a violent end — killed in a car crash during the Twenties.

In 1925 their factory was sold for 146 million dollars, and in 1928 the Chrysler Corporation bought the lot for just over 220 millions, for which they got a factory, tooling, a foundry and a name.

So what makes the Dodges of the Fifties so special?

Not a lot, unless it was names like Wayfarer, Meadowbrook and Coronet. Medium class cars with average equipment and average engines. But they did what was asked of them, i.e. sell from 250,000 to 350,000 units within a few years of the end of the Second World War.

Two important events were to bring these cars out of their anonymity and make them subjects of comparison rather than envy. Two things happened simultaneously in 1953. The first — or was it the second... no matter — was mechanical. Up till then, the Dodge bosses had always fitted their models with six cylinder engines, keeping the hemihead V8, introduced in 1951, for the top-of-the-range cars.

Unlike the Chrysler V8 with its 331 cubic inch capacity, the Dodge V8 was a kind of mini-version with 241 cu.in. called Red Ram (we still find the name Ram on present-day Dodge cars) and turning out a respectable rate for its size: 140 hp at 4400 rpm. It was optional on all models, and none too soon either, since nearly 60 per cent of all Dodges in 1953 were sold with this power unit which, so it seems, was a little marvel and as smooth as silk.

What were the true qualities of those famous Chrysler engines with their hemispherical combustion chambers? First of all, they were flexible, an important feature. Second, their construction (heads, pistons, camshaft) enabled them to turn fast and well and improved heat dissipation by the more efficient passage of coolant. Unfortunately, they were expensive to make and it was for this unhappy reason that they were frequently replaced by conventional engines of a heavier but more economical nature.

So the V8 hemi was the great innovation.

The second thing that happened was style.

Hitherto the Dodges were designed by unimaginative stylists who followed fashion rather than made it. Then in 1953 a man called Virgil Exner — formerly with Studebaker — joined Dodge as chief stylist. And things quickly began to change, not suddenly since the old-style models reappeared in 1954. But from 1955 the fins took shape that were to become wonderfully enormous in 1956 and especially in 1957.

Still, there were novelties in 1954: the Coronet, Meadowbrook and Wayfarer found a new companion, the de luxe Royal. The same year saw a Royal convertible specially prepared for Indianapolis, and 1799 Pace Car models were built and distributed to Dodge dealers, as tradition requires. In 1955 the Custom Royal Sedan retailed at 2470 dollars and the Custom Royal Lancer Hardtop at 2540 dollars.

The next year, 1956, saw a mechanical revolution when models were offered with an optional new and more powerful V8, the D-500, with a displacement of 315 cubic inches and developing 260 hp at 4600 rpm. This was a well-timed response to the mass of different versions of the Chevrolet Corvette launched in 1953,

since when every manufacturer had brought out a sports model, or at the very least an optional sports engine. From time to time extra ingredients were added to improve roadholding or braking, but these were rare enough. In 1957, the sole option was part A the suspension stiffened to withstand the extra Dodge power.

And it was precisely in 1957 that Virgil Exner's style found its full expression, with a rather violent grille, straight-line rear fenders and an overall appearance seasoned by different colour side flashes. Like all other marques, Dodge was hit by the industrial and economic crisis of 58, watching its sales drop by more than half. Unlike DeSoto however, the 59 and 60 models with their lines burning like the desert sun put the company back on the road to profit.

Dodge

1955 Royal Lancer. The grille has two cool air intakes. The dark colour did nothing to relieve the impression of weight. Note the lever to the right of the steering wheel, controlling the transmission: 55 was the only year it occupied this position

Dodge

Imperial

For Chrysler, 1950 marked the end of their in line eights and the introduction of the incredible V8 engines with hemispherical combustion chambers. This engine was fitted standard to the Crown Imperial whose code in 1951 was C-54. It was a big sedan with sombre lines and a split screen; the grille, dripping chrome, did not overwhelm the taut lines of the long hood and fenders. The rear fenders were not yet fully integral. Between 1950 and 1954 the rear window was enlarged and the rear quarter panel was given a forward sweep, a style that was adopted by a number of manufacturers who thus put an end to the restricted rear vision of the driver. There was also a long wheelbase Crown Imperial limousine. The emblem, located at the front of the hood, was a V surmounted by an imperial crown, above this was a stylised eagle's head which was given wings in 53.

But let's return in time to get a better perspective on the future. It was in 1926 that Chrysler was joined by the "Big Imperial" which took the style and image of the marque and in return was equipped with the in-line six cylinder up to 1931, when that powerful but antique unit was replaced by a big straight eight developing 125 hp and served by a four speed gearbox. Indeed for me, the Imperial is the most fantastic car ever built. A veritable monster with an outsize hood, a tiny windshield, and the whole concealed beneath a roadster form astonishing for its power and sophistication.

Even then the beast cost 3220 dollars, and for an amazing 28 years this prestige vehicle, frequently used for state occasions, made use of all the Chrysler ingredients.

By 1955 the Imperial had become a marque on its own, a de luxe vehicle still using the Chrysler stylists, assembly lines and character. Its independence was in fact necessary to separate a prestige car from a whole pack of less sophisticated vehicles. Its marque image meant that Imperial had to be out on its own and no longer just the fifth or sixth model, however refined, of a corporation turning out mass-produced automobiles.

So the Imperial was set free in 1955 to lead a life of luxury alongside Cadillac, Lincoln and Packard. That same year its styling was facelifted. The grille, now split into two, was an elegant piece of chrome-work setting off a very basic bumper. All fenders were now fully integrated into the body. Not wishing to lower itself to the level of overblown fins, Imperial overcame the problem by locating the taillights above the fender, thus preserving the pure lines and a degree of refined modesty. The Imperial, that is the standard 130 inch wheelbase model, was available as a four-door or a hardtop coupe. The engine was the 331cu.in. giving 250 hp at 4600 rpm, the same as the Crown Imperial long wheelbase of 149.5 inches.

In 1956 the car's lines are practically the same, while the 331 cubic inch engine is increased to 354 giving 280 hp at 4600 rpm. Prices were 4800 dollars for the standard model, 7700 dollars for the lwb.

In 1957, an effort at restyling was made by Virgil Exner.

Until then, the Imperial's classic looks were always just a little out of date, always a couple of years behind on its chief competitors. Whoever they were.

Cadillac held pride of place among the big luxury cars in front of Lincoln. Although the Imperial took third place, Virgil Exner aimed to recover lost ground by designing a car with really modern lines. In 1957, modernism hinged on grilles that were flat but weighed down by bumpers, and fins whose excesses had not yet attained their zenith and which were distinctly separate from the trunk lid. So the Imperial body was entirely restyled, and I am hardly exaggerating when I assert, without wading into a detailed description, that the pedigree model that came off the drawing board of Virgil Exner was the Imperial Crown Southampton Hardtop. Its new styling was typified by a huge wraparound windshield, curved windows and a rear roof pillar that looked just like a roll-over bar. The overall effect was strikingly original, clean and faultless. The little lamp which, not so long ago, hovered above the fender was now integrated in its tail.

All models were fitted with the Torque Flite automatic transmission and the engine, which was the same for all versions, was enlarged yet again. This time it was a 392 cubic inch whose power, while not excessive, was still a respectable 325 hp at 4600 rpm. The Imperial convertible was worth its 5598 dollars while the Le Baron sedan, featuring a high degree of finish and endless gadgets,

was just 4743 dollars. This slight difference was due to the type of body, the convertible being very much prized at the time.

It is worth noting here that between 1957 and 1965 the Crown Imperial Limousine was constructed by the Italian coachbuilder, Ghia. Why? There were two reasons. First because the European firm had been working with Chrysler Corporation since the early Fifties, and by 1952 was manufacturing a sports coupe named K310 based on an Exner design. This was the start of close links between Chrysler and Ghia who made several limited edition dream cars. The second reason for this decentralization was the fact that Chrysler were no longer able to justify the time spent on assembling the Imperial and the space required for it in their factories where it was more important to turn out the spearheads of the marque, DeSotos and Plymouths, at least for the time being. The big limousine was expa-

Chrysler Imperial Custom C-64 of 1954. The imperial became an independent marque from 1955

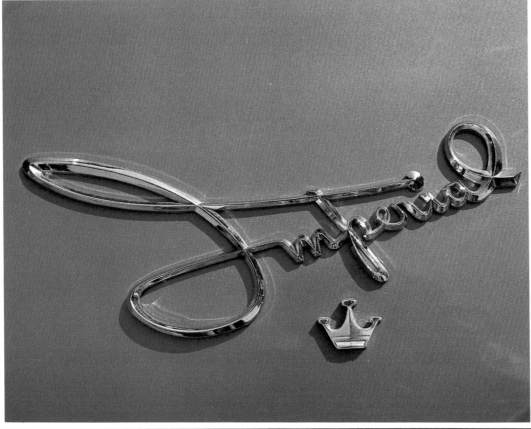

An Imperial Southampton of 1957. While the grille stayed classical with its simple grid pattern and dual headlamps, the tail went overboard: bumpers thick as steel marrows and huge fins that sported "ear probe" taillights

Imperial

triated to Italy at a stroke. The investment into constructing the car amounted to 3.3 million dollars. In order to build it, the Turin coachbuilder started with the Imperial hardtop coupe with the chassis reinforced the same the convertible. Then he cut the car in two and extended it by 20.5 inches to get the required wheelbase. This whole mechanical handling process required time and super-specialist craftsmen, all of which made the vehicle excessively expensive. While the initial price of the Imperial never went over 4800 dollars, this very special limousine retailed at the fantastic sum of 15,000! And every car took a whole month to build.

What was it all for? Where was the sense in it?

The truth is, nowhere. Because of its astronomical price, the car's sales were poor. Only 36 in 1957, 31 in 1958 and a huge 7 in 1959. Cooperation between Chrysler and Ghia continued on into 1965, when total production of the Crown type stood at 132 units.

As for the short wheelbase Imperials, 1957 was their best year ever: 38,000 vehicles sold, taking the Imperial to second place just behind Cadillac but beating Lincoln for the first (and last) time.

We now jump two years: by 1959 the Imperial's lines were practically unaltered, only a few details of the grille and decor made any difference. The real improvements came from beneath, from the mechanics. The car was fitted with air suspension on the front wheels. While retaining its Torque Flite auto transmission, it featured a so-called Full Time power steering. Under the hood, the engine had grown yet again, and was now a massive 413 cubic inches generating 350 hp at 4600 rmp without a murmur. Henceforth, this heavy car would become a fast car, attaining 100 mph in 19 seconds, pretty frightening for 2.2 tons of hurtling metal. Not to mention the brakes which when applied vigorously showed a great talent for fading.

At this point I must make note of a

The mountainous profile of the 1961 Imperial. The rear roof section ot this pillarless 4-door was reminiscent of a landau

four-door monster, a sort of automotive degeneracy that was called the 1961 Crown Imperial. The one I saw near San Diego was red, the property of a decent fellow of 45 who collects Imperials — he owns five! I took an instant liking to the red one. Perfectly restored, it simply breathed luxury and spaciousness. Its styling is far from the relative purity of the 57 model. While the grille has been kept simple, the four headlamps are no longer an integral part of the bodywork but have "leapt out" from the fender in a way reminiscent of the Thirties. The roof is classical and simple but the immense rear fins, sharp as needles, lend the car a terrifying and monstrous aspect. The rear bumper is oddly split. The engine is still the 413 cu.in. developing its 350 hp, and was to continue giving excellent service down to 1965. So far then, no innovations, no surprises.

The dashboard on the other hand bears witness to an undisputed search for perfection. To begin with, the steering wheel is not quite round, the "top and bottom" are flattened.

Then there is the dial cluster proper, reflecting much research and perfect originality. The most strikingly original feature are the two groups of buttons, one either side of the wheel. On the left are the buttons that control the auto transmission. To the right, headlamps, screen wipers and all servo equipment. Quite apart from the unique stylishness of this panel, one fact stands out: it is totally functional, since it is possible to activate each button by fingertip touch without taking the hand off the wheel. This was a true revolution for its day and came long before the same feature was built into the Citroën CX fifteen years later, and that is a car we like to call revolutionary, particularly in this very area.

When it comes to cars, the Americans have done it all before.

Front end of the 61, showing refined grille but fenders looking like cut-down plane wings

Imperial

The 1961 Imperial in colour. Note the fin shaped like a suppository (for a horse) and the "stuck-on" front and rear lights just like in the Twenties. The emblem was naturally an (Imperial) eagle

Imperial

Plymouth

The Plymouth and DeSoto marques have a lot in common. First, they became part of the Chrysler Corporation in the same year, 1928. Second, they were seen by the public as being reliable and sensible cars synonymous with value for money. Finally, and this is where we come in, the Fifties were to mark their bodies with crazy fins and grilles as heavy as slabs of cast iron. Unlike DeSoto, Plymouth easily rode out the crisis of 1958 and continued its tranquil existence on into the present.

At the dawn of the Fifties the Plymouth was hampered by a major drawback: its cars were not fitted with the V8 despite its belonging to the Chrysler Corporation which at that time possessed the 331. The poor things had to wait till 1955 to experience real joy in the shape of a small 260 cubic inch unit that developed 157 hp or optionally 167 hp. Not exactly Paradise, but better than nothing. The more so since, from the end of the war, the Plymouth stylists did not exactly excel themselves. They changed styles when they felt like it, and always after everyone else had thought of it, and even then

their designs were of a deliberate banality as if stressing the ordinariness of the car.

This rather unhealthy preface gives you the flavour of Plymouth. From 1955 onwards the image changed, becoming less rigid. This in turn was due to the new engine as well as to a new body which, while not over-original, was nevertheless modern. With a low waistline and a simple grille, the back was without the fins you would have expected to have seen in 1954 in the form of ridiculous chrome appendages stuck unfortunately on the wing and not integral to the design.

Inside there were none of the push buttons controlling the transmission that were found on the Chryslers. Transmission was by means of a stock lever mounted centrally in the instrument panel and which one simply moved up or down.

It was obvious that neither 1955 nor 1956 were not — yet — the years of glory for the Plymouth. Still, 1956 did witness a promising future. The cars were restyled, and though the front end is oddly reminiscent of the 55 models, the back was already showing a desire to reach for the sky. This was the start of Plymouth fins, and it was a clean start enhanced by appropriate side mouldings. This was the brand new Fury which supplemented the series of Belvedere, Savoy and Plaza. The new Fury, an aggressive name that featured for a long time in the Plymouth catalogue, also sported a new V8 of 303 cubic inches developing 240 and 270 hp.

It is important to mention these innovations since the marque was generally miserly with them, seeking to construct a truly well-selling machine rather than a dream car or competition vehicle. This is why the Plymouth prices were the lowest in the Chrysler range. Leaving aside the Chrysler and Imperial marques, here are some examples that speak volumes. In 1950 the basic price of a DeSoto was 1996 dollars, for a Dodge 1629 dollars and for a Plymouth, 1386 dollars. In 1955, the

Not beautiful but certainly appealing: the 1950 Plymouth sedan (background) and wagon

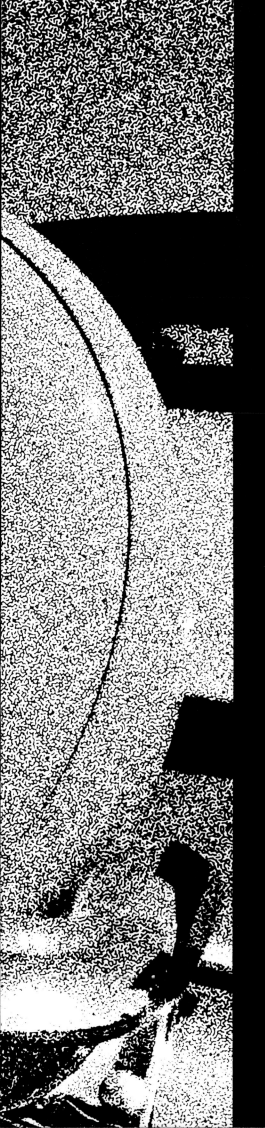

FORD MOTOR CO.

The 58 Edsel, the first of the marque, had by far the most original front end of the Fifties. But the car was a commercial failure. Rear fenders had gull-wing styling. Note pushbutton transmission controls in steering wheel hub and drum speedometer. Certainly a stylish automobile!

Edsel

Edsel

The motives that prompt a human being to collect things are many, varied and often obscure. It may be the accomplishment of an old dream.

The pleasure of possession or of hoarding. Of being seen, showing off. Of being the only one to have one... Everyone has his reasons and his interests. But these days who can understand anyone wanting to own an Edsel? Can you imagine anyone wanting to raise the *Titanic* and make it even better than before?

The Edsel was the *Titanic* of the American motor industry. Chrysler had their Airflow that made all America laugh. This time, 1958, it was Ford's turn to be made fun of, to have a flop with a car which, after all is said and done, was not all that bad to look at.

The Edsel was an unprecedented failure that is hard to explain, though every kind of explanation has been given, written, spoken, even sung. Some say the styling was no good. Others, that the medium range car market was finished. Or the year was not a good one. That the car had

The profile of the 58 Edsel was the car's only classical feature

poor roadholding. It was run down so much that it became an incredible failure, reflected by sales of 63,000 units in 58, 45,000 in 59 and a meagre 3000 in 60! It has been said that the name Edsel was a mistake (Ford management hired a poet named Marianne Moore who came up with 6000 names!). Jean Rosenbaum, a doctor of psychiatry, has stated that the appearance of the Edsel was displeasing from a strictly emotional and psychological viewpoint, the vertical grille resembling a huge gaping mouth. Personally, I wonder whether this Puritan wasn't thinking of something else. Be that as it may, the poor car never recovered, and that is why I repeat the question: who could possibly want to collect Edsels after all that?

Admittedly, the Edsel collectors are few and far between. A large number of the cars were destroyed and the fervent Edsel fans like to keep themselves to themselves. For them, this was an intriguingly rare vehicle and one powerful enough to do 0-60 in 9.7 seconds, at least with its big mill. The most original of the Edsels was undoubtedly the 58 model, which featured the celebrated optional extra with the name of "Teletouch Electric Push Button Transmission Selector". Its engineers wanted a car that was unique, astonishing and attractive right down to its smallest detail at

any price. In fact the Teletouch was nothing more than a pushbutton auto selector, but located in the steering wheel hub! A crazy idea that made people die laughing. The first instrument panel was truly "in" with its circular speedometer (just like on the Citroën CX).

A disappearing aerial was featured, also a remotely opened trunk lid. This mid-class car incorporated maximum gadgetry to appeal to the broad mass of the American population who were further spoiled for choice between three different wheelbases. The 124 inch wheelbase was reserved for the more expensive models like the Corsair and the Citation; the inbetween wheelbase (118 inches) for the Pacer and the Ranger, while the shortest (116) was for the wagons. The top-of the-line model was the Citation convertible. Quite apart from its very special front end, the car's rear quarters reflected a touch of modesty compared with the Dodges and Plymouths of the same age. The eyebrow-shaped lamps surmount a respectable bumper that is nothing to write home about. As for the engine — noblesse oblige — no straight here, but a choice of two V8s, both amenable engines, the 361 cubic inch developing 303 hp and the 410 turning out 345 hp.

In spite of its trump cards, Ford soon realized that the Edsel was not selling. The Pacer was deleted in 1959 alongside the Citation and all the wagons with the exception of the Villager. In addition, the options now included a straight six of 145 hp, while two new V8s with lower power ratings now made their debut: the 292 (200 hp) and the 332 (225 hp); the existing 361 cu.in. was retained.

1959 saw a lot of changes, and many attempts were made to put the train back on the rails. But it was a hopeless case; sales continued to fall despite a facelifted grille and a somewhat calmer rear end. The Teletouch of course had disappeared — what idiot wanted to change gear when he thought he was honking his horn! 1960 models were as ugly as their

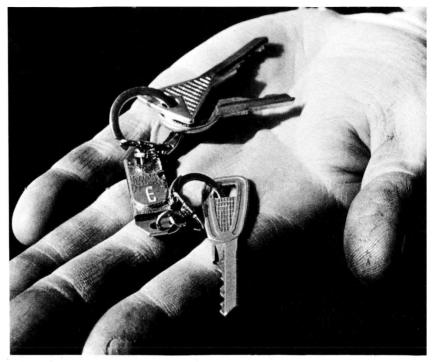

predecessors, and still Ford's management tried to get things under control. The vertical grille, a veritable horror in the eyes of the masses, was replaced for ever by a straight grille reminiscent of the Pontiac. The rear end was almost the same as the Fairlane but with vertical, not horizontal, lights. The Edsel became so plain that it lost its true character as well as some fans that had remained true to its deranged look. This time around, in 1960, there were just two models, the two and four door Ranger and the Villager wagon, all of which spelled certain death and disaster, while the power units were also locked in this ever-decreasing circle. The 410 cubic inch big block had long since disappeared, leaving a straight six of 145 hp, two V8s, the 292 and 185 hp, plus the 300 horsepower 352 cu.in.

At that time the Ranger retailed at 2635 dollars, a reasonable price indeed. Sadly enough though, no one wanted this car any more — it was just too laughable, too ridiculous. And so Ford put a stop to the Edsel massacre in November 1960. But let not the Edsel fans despair! Their favourite car had a lot of talent. And if they don't know exactly why they collect it, so what? The main thing is that this many-flawed machine has endured.

Even the keys echoed the shape of the grille (58 only). In fact, the grille design was reprised in no fewer than seven decor and trim features

Edsel

At left *The 59 model of the Edsel, with grille restyled for more conventionality. Styling of the 1960 model* (this page) *was modest, making it a kind of Fairlane. Production of the Edsel stopped in November 1960*

Edsel

Ford

If you asked me to count all the car clubs in California it would take more than a whole day. According to official Los Angeles statistics, there are around 400 clubs of all kinds in this sun-drenched state of the US. The fact is that the states of the West and Middle West are blessed by the climate, and it is more tempting to bring out a collector's car there than in the East.

This remarkable fact stems from the need to congregate. Whatever his social condition, the American belongs to one or more clubs. Why? The answer is easy. Since the early frontier days, in the wide-open spaces and tough pioneer conditions, men always got together in the face of danger, a kind of reflex that modern man retains deep down in his innermost being. Like a subconscious form of defence. The least excuse is enough to show off his car, to seek out his soul mates.

Naturally, all talk is of engines and gearboxes, but the important thing is to get together in a warm, safe atmosphere. A world where everyone knows his place and problems just do not exist. Men will travel hundreds of miles just to feel this animal warmth, this peace of mind. So what if he is driving a car that's 50 years old? He knows that it will get him there, and once he has arrived, a few beers in good company will obliterate his fatigue.

We were told of a Fifties Ford meet held two hours from San Francisco. They said it would be a remote spot among the pines, forgetting to tell us the exact location. Once in Virginia City, we began our search for the place: not the slightest trace of a Ford. We asked pump attendants, hotels, even the local sheriff, but no one had seen as much as a Ford fender. Surely you'd notice a 50 or 55 Ford wouldn't you? Things like that you notice.

We eventually discovered these great people quite by chance, hidden away in a motel. Now motels are usually laid out in a U-shape, which was why we could not see the cars — they were hiding inside the U!

Still, the detour was worth it. My God what a party! They were all there, old 48s, jolly 50s, frenzied 58s. And the amazing thing, apart from all that paintwork glistening and shimmering in the sunshine, was that most of the owners were ten or twenty years older than their cars; this accurately reflects the make-up of collectors of current automobiles. Fords? The streets are full of them, so are the classified ads with reasonable prices (though a 50 convertible still fetches 10,000 dollars), so you don't drive these cars for the glory of it or to impress the onlookers. You buy a modest Ford or Mercury because you dreamed about one when you were 12 years old or because your Dad had one. A touching gesture.

The cars were truly in immaculate condition. I dare you to find such a gathering of similar cars in England, of Hillmans, for example. And you tell me if they are good enough to put in a showroom pretending to be the latest model. In the States, they don't just patch up cars, they remake them. The first one that struck me — without hurting me — was a 1948 convertible that I started to ogle. Not a particularly enticing automobile, but in such good shape that my jaw dropped. Its owner was a little older than the rest, around 45. He told me it was second-hand and that the car was all original. And since he knew it all by heart he began to run through the history of the marque. I have to admit that the Ford story is not exactly studded with great moments, at least not since 1903. It was in that year that Henry Ford senior set up his factory. The next chapter in the Ford story came from 1908 to 1927, the era of the Model T, superseded by the Ford A. The third milestone was the birth in 1932

The really attractive 1948 Ford Convertible had warm, rounded lines. The instrument panel was comprehensive and well-arranged. It had a 3-speed manual shift

Ford

The number plate on this Ford says it all: the most beautiful and sought-after model was the 1950, especially the convertible, its current value being around 10,000 dollars. Opposite *Front and side views of the very elegant Fairlane Crown Victoria two-door coupe*

Ford

of the famous V8. The fourth and last "event" before my 48 convertible was the integration of headlamps into the fenders in 1937.

Not much to go on it's true, but still! With his robust, durable products, Henry Ford made cars that were hard to get away from. Reliable? Not quite down to the very last detail perhaps, but he built cars that were simple, which means easy to repair.

Which is why the 48 convertible I'm looking at right now had a plainness that bordered on the antique. No independent suspension, not even in 1948 (?), no power steering or assisted brakes, just the V8 with five more horsepower: 90 in 1946 and 95 in 1948. That's progress for you! Outside, the car is sparse on looks. It is high and relatively narrow. Its austere impression is not helped by a grille that ends before the headlamps. Inside it's a different story, with room for five persons in comfort. The dashboard comprised two large dials located either side of the chromed loudspeaker, while four little rectangular gauges recorded engine data.

I had to tell you about this car because right after it came a major switch in policy, a rare enough event at Ford. Among the great moments in Ford's history, I forgot to mention one important one: unlike its competitors, Ford had introduced the V8 before the six cylinder that came out in 1941.

In 1949 an entirely new model was presented to the press. This was the Tudor (two-door) and Fordor (four-door). Although the windshield was still split, the styling innovations were many. A unit body that came in three sizes, integral fenders and a front end that looked like an airplane. Above all else, contemporary stylists wanted to copy the airplane, or at least borrow some of its features like fins and nose, as we see one year later with Studebaker but with a lot more effectiveness. The new Ford had independent front suspension on coil springs, a Hotchkiss rigid rear axle on semi-ellipticals; steering was revised to become more direct, while the engine was the by then venerable side valve V8 that had hardly changed since 1932. The shift stayed manual with three forward speeds, but a Borg-Warner overdrive came as an optional extra. There were no changes for 1950 except for a few styling details and the appearance of a de luxe version, the Crestliner.

The cars were to undergo slight variations down the passing years but with no major facelifts. Styling gently followed current fashion. In 1951 there was a new grille and revamped rear quarter panel — this was the Victoria. The rear end remained practically unchanged. Mechanically, the engine was nearly untouched. A marvellous automatic transmission was introduced, the Ford-O-Matic, the very first of Ford's auto boxes. An event, yes, but still behind all the others and which passed quite unheeded.

Come 1953 and Ford's fiftieth birthday. You could be forgiven for thinking that Ford would have wanted to bring out a completely new model, something modern on all counts — not at all. Henry was a man of habit: same body as the previous year, same chassis. It was in fact all the same car as usual, except for two things.

And this time the change were marked, major decisions had been taken with determination. Power steering — Master Guide — was available as an extra but only on cars fitted with the V8. This was a revolution.

But beside what was still to come, the power steering looked pretty old hat: the ancient side valve V8 first made its appearance in 1932 — remember? — was replaced by a V8 with overhead valves. In its initial guise, this power pack provided 130 hp for a capacity of 239 cubic inches. It was introduced in 1954 and was accompanied by a new straight six especially for those with a smaller pocket but with a capacity almost the same as the V8, developing 115 hp out of 223 cu.in. The

Ford

1956 Fairlane two-door coupe was hardly changed over the 55 model. The Crown Victoria had the 225 hp engine of the T-Bird

Ford

1958 Fairlane Skyliner showing various stages in hardtop retract. The only problem was that, with the hardtop stowed, the trunk was full! Note how hardtop front section folds back. Opposite The same model in 1959, called the Galaxie Skyliner

Ford

models were called the Crestline Sunliner and Crestline Victoria. At last there was a very nice Ford — the Skyliner for the modest sum of 2199 dollars. This vehicle was fitted with the V8 and for an extra 134 dollars you could have a transparent Perspex roof. At that time, 1954, Fords were becoming rather less austere under the influence of tough competition and were offering five major options. First was power steering with 75 per cent assistance. Second were power brakes that relieved the driver of two-thirds of his foot effort.

Then there was automatic transmission, of course. Next came electric windows, and finally there was an electrically four-way adjustable front seat: forward, rear, up and down.

All of which brings us fairly and squarely out of the Thirties, those wonderful years when a change of door handle was sufficient to make a new model. In 1955 Ford followed the trend to straight lines, straight body waists and nascent fins by presenting a totally re-cast range. Grilles were now side and low-slung, devoid of triviality and excess and still retaining a measure of finesse.

The Ford arms with its three stylized lions

For this attractive new range the Detroit manufacturer offered six new V8 engines with capacities and ratings to suit everyone. Chassis underwent a slight rejuvenation of detail. The facts that are worth noting include a redesigned line for the Fairlane Victoria and above all the new, young Fairlane Sunliner.

The Fairlanes when they emerged had a stroke of luck — they were fitted with the T-bird engine, 272 cubic inches, a four-barre carburettor, separate dual exhausts and an 8.5: 1 compression. This combination produced 185 horsepower at full throttle, and to give the driver a better view of the road, especially when he hammered down, the cars were now fitted with a panoramic windshield that came in for an awful lot of criticism. While its main surface afforded perfect forward vision, the side wraps distorted visibility and encroached on the doors.

By comparison, 1956 was a calm year. The calm before the storm being prepared in the depths of Ford's offices. Front-end lines remained unchanged except for a few details. Only the Fairlane was entitled to a substantial facelift. Its V8 was boosted to 292 cubic inches developing 202 horsepower at a compression ratio of 8.4:1. For Ford, this year of transition was to be their year of safety: brakes were beefed up steering revised and suspension better matched so as to withstand increased engine power without tears. The convertible, the Victoria, Crown Victoria and Skyliner were still part of the Ford range, although the Skyliner's time had come, and you will soon see why. Only 600 cars of this type were sold in 1956 which made it hardly worthwhile.

Elsewhere, Ford were preparing a car that would revolutionize 1957. This was the Fairlane Skyliner with retractable hardtop, a most attractive automobile whose production under the name of Skyliner Galaxie was to cease in 1959.

What was so special about it? First, the 57 styling was completely facelifted, with less rigid lines, headlamps that wore a kind of kidney-cutter, and round taillights topped by pointed fins that started somewhere along the sides. Ford's great achievement was to follow the fin fashion without going over the top. But the Fairlane Skyliner was really something else. It had a roof which, once retracted into the trunk, transformed the vehicle into a true convertible. Everything was electric, and the roof mechanism worked something like this: 1) the trunk lid opened front first; 2) the hardtop lifted; 3) before dropping into the trunk, the front section of the roof folded down; 4) the roof dropped into the trunk; 5) finally the lid closed again with its front section extended to close the gap left by the roof. All this was great except for one thing with the hard top in the trunk, it was full up with no room left for so much as a beach towel. Secondly, this mechanical marvel was rather delicate; the whole system relied on hydraulic rams, worm gears and electric drive which, after twenty years of excellent service, often break down. It wasn't for nothing that the owner of the 58 Skyliner shown in these pages told us: "You're in luck — it all works. Sometimes the whole shebang jams halfway." This magical automobile came out at 2942 dollars fitted with a new V8 giving 245 hp out of 312 cubic inches. The complex roof mechanism made the model just 400 dollars cheaper than the T-Bird, but it was a car that pleased a lot of people. Nearly 20,000 of them were made in 1957. In 1958 only 14,713 Fairlane 500 Skyliners were sold, while sales figures for the Galaxie Skyliner fell to 12,915 by 1959. When you think that it was trunkless with the roof down and very "unconvertible" with a full trunk, these figures are not too bad. Still, this kind of very special car soon loses its novelty: customers gradually lost interest and production ceased compltely on thc vcrgc of the Sixties.

Up to 1964 the Galaxies, Fairlanes and Victoria only retained one thing in common — their round taillights!

Next page *The wonderful Fairlane 500 convertible of 1957. To mark Ford's fiftieth anniversary (1907) it was fitted with a 245 hp V8*

Ford

71

Lincoln

There is a story told about the Lincoln. I cannot say how true it is but I shall still tell it, for good stories make friends.

It happened in 1940. Edsel Ford, son of the great Henry, was to spend a few days' vacation in Florida. To make his stay even better it was decided to build him a unique car. This was a design which the stylists had been working on for over a year but which nobody really liked very much. Still, the car was beautiful and elegant, so they made a running prototype which, once complete, astonished Edsel, his companions and the Ford directors.

Instantly the decision was changed, and the car was manufactured in small numbers to become the prestige image of the marque.

And that was how the Lincoln Continental was born. At least according to the story, written in 1940.

I have to confess that I have no great attraction for the car. Basically its front quarters were those of the 40 Ford. The windscreen was straight and the fenders very heavy. What apparently gave the car its style was the visible spare wheel. Subsequently, Ford proposed the optional "Continental" kit (Mercury) which consisted precisely of the spare wheel on the back of the trunk and an extended bumper.

I do not intend to squander these pages on this car — it belongs fairly and squarely to the Forties, not to the Fifties. Nevertheless I will say a few words about it so you know what to look for if ever you should want one one day.

Its production ran from 1940 to 1948 during which time the body was facelifted several times, not always a good idea since as the modifications multiplied, especially those to the grille, the car got to resemble nothing so much as a rather stylish iron. Then there was the engine.

When it appeared in 1940 the Lincoln Continental was powered by the old V12 which had been fitted to the Lincoln Zephyr in the Thirties. This was a 292 cubic inch putting out a modest 120 hp.

The trouble with this mill was that it was a total disaster — never had such a production engine been so badly designed before. It's a wonder the public ever accepted it. The V12 was delicate with a fragility that went deep down inside it. First, it overheated. Then it was poorly splash lubricated so that it shot its big ends whenever you pushed it to top speed. It was better not to buy it and wait for 1942 when it was at last decided to scrap it. It was replaced by another V12 that was not much bigger : 303 cubic inches for 120 horsepower, but it was at least tough and reliable.

This car, Ford's de luxe model, cost 4474 dollars in 1946, 4746 in 1947 and 1948, for both coupe and convertible. Few units were made : 466 in 1946, 1560 in 1947 and 1300 in 1948.

I shall begin the Fifties with the Cosmopolitan, a round, bulbous automobile in a Ford tradition that was to extend to the Mercury models (we will see why). At the dawn of the Fifties the engines were still pretty poor affairs and the unhappy Lincolns crept around like snails. Ironically, they had names like Sport Sedan, Cosmopolitan Sport Sedan and Cosmopolitan Capri, which did nothing to help their image.

Their lumps and bumps paralleled the image of their engines : the overall effect was sloppy. In 1952, thank God, the car changed its face and its engine. Gone were the insipid bulges and the tired engines. The new totally redesigned V8 was a 317 cubic inch developing 160 horsepower (205 in 1953), quite a respectable rating bearing in mind the competition : Cadillac and Chrysler. With its 205 hp the Lincoln had 0.64 hp for every cubic inch against the Cadillac's 0.63 and the Chrysler's 0.54.

These few statistics serve to show that Ford was getting back on top after being rather out of touch towards the end of the Forties. This time power was accompanied by great toughness amply demonstrated in Panamerican road races that were popular at the time (Los Angeles to Mexico). While the car won places of honour and took first and second in 1954. this was not due to its intrinsic power but to outstanding preparation by a man called Clay Smith who sadly died soon after; with a tall rear axle the Lincoln attained its 130 mph top speed, an astonishing achievement.

But don't get the wrong idea : Lincolns were never competition cars. The race preparation and the results it achieved were exceptional. The production vehicle was quite different, being designed, manufactured and sold to offer maximum comfort, a high degree of safety, and was intended to compete with the Cadil-

lacs and Packards, doing battle on finish and interior detail.

There were plenty of innovations at the start of the Fifties. Rubber bushing was introduced onto front suspensions making for extra comfort and smoothness. Unlike other manufacturers, the Lincoln's brake drums were oversized for added safety. The power steering had ball-race mechanics which, though unique, was not especially precise. The wheelbase of the Capri and Cospopolitan was just 123 inches which means that the car's length was not excessive bearing in mind its intended image. Still, interior space was adequate mainly due to a commonsense-sized-trunk (unlike the Cadillac). The driver's seat was electrically adjustable in four different ways. Noise insulation was greatly enhanced. Models equipped with Ford air conditioning also had induced ventilation just in case the air conditioning system failed.

What sophistication! The cars were

The mid-Fifties saw the birth of a spectacular car of simple, serene lines: the 56-57 Lincoln Continental. This is the Mark II, 300 horsepower model that came out at close to 10,000 dollars.
Next page The "Continental Kit" outside spare disappeared to make way for a larger trunk lid that looked rather like...

Lincoln

much prized despite their ugliness; for you have to admit that their lines look like nothing in particular. The styling was soft and unimaginative, and history managed to erase them gently and peacefully without anyone getting overly upset.

Today, buffs of early Fifties Continentals are few and far between. Lincoln fans prefer.... Well, what do they prefer? The Continental Mark II that came out in 1956. And they were not wrong either.

So here we are with the Mark II. The car's design was entrusted to Henry Ford II's youngest brother, William Clay, When he saw the first sketches, the indulgent big brother said "I wouldn't put a dime on it." Affable words putting the recipient in a good frame of mind. I have no idea what those early sketches looked like, but all the same, the end result was great. An American might say : "Great man, great."

It was an immense coupe (only one convertible was built) with a particularly long, low hood. The whole car was low-slung, with an attractively rounded but not panoramic windshield, and a trunk with the mock impression of a spare wheel. The overall effect was truly interesting, so much so that this 1956 model could not be compared to other Lincolns, whose excesses and stylistic irrationality were incomprehensible. The Mark II was twenty years ahead of its time. Today it attracts buffs eager to see and appreciate but reluctant to buy. A specimen in perfect condition could fetch between 25,000 and 40,000 dollars, figures that reflect its rarity and classic good looks. Even the front end is free from flights of chrome-plated fancy; I personally would have liked to see the bumper a little lighter, but at the time it was well liked. The engine turned out nothing less than 300 hp — a V8 which was still pretty slender to haul the car's 2.4 tons. For all its overall good impression and original instrument panel, William Clay's car was not long-lived and spent hardly two years on the market. The reason? Its price.

The price was exorbitant to say the least. In 1957 for instance, a Lincoln Capri (bottom of the line up) cost 4649 dollars; the Premiere Convertible stood at 5381 dollars while the Mark II came in at nearly 10,000 dollars — 9358 in 1956. No wonder

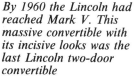

By 1960 the Lincoln had reached Mark V. This massive convertible with its incisive looks was the last Lincoln two-door convertible

orders were scarce. 2200 takers in two years was not many. The car's high price was the result of production processes : it was expensive to make by virtue of its sumptuous fittings and above-average interior and exterior finish. Be that as it may, there is no denying that the monster had ten times the charm of the latter Mark I which had become so bloated and disfigured by its chrome But the Mark II never even had a chance to grow old gracefully — the price of glory unsupported by sales.

In 1958 this automobile was superseded by the Continental Mark III. While the Mark I had aged badly, and the Mark II was short-lived, the Mark III had the misfortune to even exist : it was an abominable flop — a flat monster whose panels were just asking to be scratched. The only redeeming feature was a simple grille up front. Otherwise, there were quad headlamps halfway out of bed, bullet bumper bars that ended at the side in a kind of fishtail, and everything else to match. Admittedly, the quality was there and the Mark III was the longest car with 229 inches bumper-to-bumper. Its 430 cubic inch engine was the biggest of the day, generating 375 horsepower; believe me, they need all that cavalry to shift to hulk of metal with any dignity at all. Let's get one thing straight : so as not to repeat the commercial catastrophe of the Mark II, the styling of the Mark III was almost identical to the Capri. Almost. The exceptions were details like the electric rear window (inverted). By these means Ford succeeded in cutting substantially the price of the car which, in 1958, retailed at no more than 6283 dollars. All of which did not stop total sales for that year from dropping to 25,000 from 41,000 the year before.

Right up to the end of 1960 the Lincolns all retained their tortured line, add-ons, angular, truncated shapes, and the inverted rear window (only on the Continental Mark V). Once rid of its roof, the convertible took on a decent appearance. The bumpers were restyled and the

sides thankfully lost their metal trim. The instrument panel was well-designed : four big dials showed the status of engine and other units. As for the engine, it retained its 430 cubic inches but power was downgraded to 315 hp. Prices for the Lincoln Premiere, the Town Car, the Continental and the Limousine ranged from 5253 to 10,230 dollars.

From 1961 up to 1965 — how times change — the Lincoln Continental was totally redesigned, and with real artistry! With its extra-clean lines, nickel grille and almost invisible bumpers. The most attractive windshield design was also used for the convertible — yes, they made a four-door convertible too. Today, perfect specimens are rare indeed and their value can only increase. Up to 1963 the Continental's wheelbase was 123 inches but from 1964 right down to 1969 it was stretched to 126 inches to make the rear seating more spacious. In 1961 the 430 cubic inches developed 300 hp while power was raised to 320 hp in 1965.

Amazingly enough, the convertible, which was capable of attaining an effortless 125 mph, did not make the least interior noise at high speed. Everything was constructed with thorough, minute precision and attention to detail.

For the roof, the engineers had adopted the Fairlane Skyliner system which meant that the electric deck opened front-to-rear and the roof, also electric, settled nicely into the trunk. The car had a unit body and disc brakes at the front. These were necessary to stop the two-and-a-half-tons-plus of the convertible in full flight, though a couple more wouldn't have done any harm! Aside from the 320 horsepower aided by an inverted Carter four-barrel, we find a Twin-Range Turbo Drive auto transmission with three forward speeds. Indeed the only weak spot of the car was its rigid rear axle hung simply on rather pathetic semi-elliptics. In 1965 it cost 6930 dollars. So let's forgive and forget.

Lincoln

The new Lincoln
Continental finally
appeared in 1961, with
extremely clean,
straight-through lines.
Shown here is the 65
model with only grille and
tail facelifted. It featured
contra-opening doors and
a drophead that
disappeared into the trunk

Lincoln

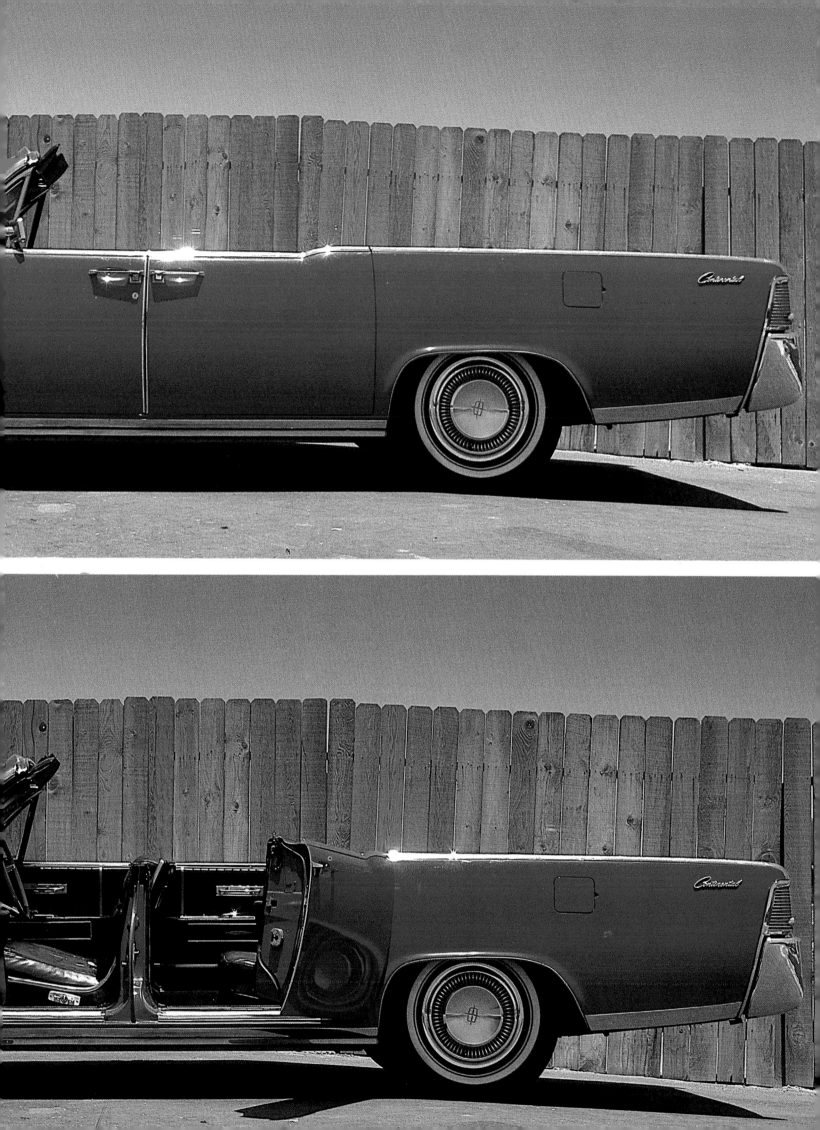

Mercury

They say it is getting hard to do a good deal on old cars in Europe. Finding your dream car in pristine condition, hidden away in some barn for years like a mechanical Sleeping Beauty — these things just don't happen any more. Embalmed beneath straw, well preserved from the weather, just 6000 miles from new — a pipedream. Just blow off the dust, hand a few pounds to the owner who is naturally ignorant of its true value — what a laugh. Turn the key, bid farewell to the poor sap that sold it to you, and glide easily out on the main road. Plain wishful thinking.

Likewise, it would be silly to think such things happened in the States either, bearing in mind the number of cars. Over there you just have to open up a copy of *Hemmings* (a magazine specializing in classified ads, with twenty pages of Cadillacs and fifty of Fords every month) and pick out the car of your choice. No, these things don't happen any more. Mind you, you do find beautiful specimens at affordable prices, but if you're talking about a really superb example with brilliant paintwork despite its age and only 6000 on the clock, you're talking tens of thousands of dollars.

Nevertheless, I did meet the man and the car that were the exceptions to the rule: a nice old guy, a Basque by origin but a resident of California, who owned a super-splendid dark blue 1946 Mercury drophead that had done 5000 miles from new. It was a marvellous story, since not only was the car in mint condition, he had bought it from an old Hollywood star who for some shady reason suddenly wanted to be rid of a vehicle she had lovingly kept for thirty years. That's how they are, movie stars, impulsive. What a stroke of luck for the old man! And

I'd swear that the convertible was new. It was so incredible, it was incredible! Especially since a Mercury is not just any car; the 46 may well have looked like a twin to the 46 Ford, but it was on a superior level. The Mercury belonged to the middle-class while the Ford, let's face it, was a low-flier. A 1946 Mercury Woody convertible cost 2078 dollars, while the equivalent Ford fetched 1865. The difference was in the finish, the power and all the little things that lent a touch of class; Ford's plain grille was half as expensive as the Mercury's, attractively laden with chrome and of sophisticated design.

Overall, the two cars looked as though they had come out of the same factory. To look at them you know they are made by the same firm. What could be more normal?

Why, you are probably wondering, is he going on about these two dropheads so persistently. I'll tell you. Because it stayed that way right up to 1948. Then, the two sisters took totally different stylistic roads.

And the reason? I shall attempt to explain, but it won't be easy, so try to concentrate and open your mind. After the war, Ford had a project on the drawingboard for a 118-inch wheelbase Mercury. Then it was decided that this car would be the new Ford for 1949. The only question was, what would the 49 Mercury look like now that its design had been stolen? At the same time, there was a project for a Lincoln with a wheelbase of 121 inches which was a bit short for a prestige car. So to make things nice and tidy the Lincoln project became the new Mercury for 1949, while the 49 Lincoln Cosmopolitan with the 125-inch wheelbase became the 49 Lincoln Zephyr which, as it turned out, never saw the light of day.

Hence the difference. On the one hand was the Ford and its original design, on the other the Mercury that looked just like a Lincoln. Clear as mud, isn't it!

This Mercury, manufactured from 1949 to 1951, was to become a

legend by virtue of its curvaceous shape, a certain rotundity that is not unpleasant. The front end was ornamented with a sweet little chromed cylindrical grille, headlamps were nicely integral, while the rear quarters, so often sinfully over-the-top in those days, were rounded but well-proportioned. The vehicle came in a four-door version, a very beautiful coupe, a convertible and a woody wagon. In 1949 a Mercury sedan would set you back 1997 dollars, while a Ford with its meagre straight six engine was just 1333. The difference got bigger too, so much so in fact that the old V8 of 239 cubic inches grew, soon passing the 255 cu. in. mark. Power also increased and leapt (or was it crept?) by 10 hp to 110 in all. Prior to the 49 model, Mercurys had transverse spring suspension front and rear. But now things were different: front wheels were on coil springs and the rear rigid axle on semi-elliptics.

It has to be said that Edsel Ford who was managing the project had envisaged independent suspension all-round, an idea that horrified his father Henry who supervised the affair and who, after all, was as "careful" as a whole army of Scotsmen. Careful, but nevertheless a good bookkeeper. He knew better than anyone that all-round independent suspension would have been unprofitable. To Hell with comfort! Cash comes first. Production cars had a three-speed manual box with on optional two-speed auto transmission with the "touching" name of Touch-O-Matic.

In 1950 there appeared a new model, the Monterey coupe for six passengers that featured a vinyl covered roof. This car, by the way, was selected to be the official Pace Car for the Indianapolis 500. In 1951 there were few changes to upset the pleasing lines of the Mercury: a new grille and a few new details. The Touch-O-Matic transmission was fitted standard and its V8 now sported 112 horsepower. The Mercury's performance was not exactly spectacular

Mercury

Two 1950 Mercury convertibles in perfect condition. The blue one had added foglamps and searchlights that could be aimed from inside. The dashboard echoed the grille design

Mercury

and was close to that of a 1939 model. It has to be said that the engine had progressed too slowly and was out of touch with buyer's expectations; with a semi-de luxe car you want some response under your right foot. Which was why, in 1952, the car had a V8 developing 125 hp in an all-new body redesigned in the manner of a Ford, not a Lincoln. This time, the bulges had disappeared as if by magic. The car was square, or almost. The clearly straight grille emphasized the severe and precise front end, while the screen was no longer split. As for the rear quarters, they started halfway down the car, falling to canted taillights which in turn transitioned smoothly into the rear bumper. It was a body that concealed new, sweet-smelling surprises. The 52 version lost 200 pounds to the old model. Steering and brakes were now power assisted, while the driver's seat became electrically adjustable. The main and magical innovation was the new dashboard with its aviation flavour: in the centre, a semicircular speedometer with the four standard dials for water temperature, fuel, oil pressure and battery status. Either side of the big main dial were four small handles you could push or pull. These were for controlling fresh air ventilation. Automatic transmission was controlled from a small stick to the right

of the steering column on which a small indicator lamp showed the driver which drive he had selected. Further right, the dash panel continued across the car with clock, ashtray and radio. I drove this car for a few miles and found that its special qualities lay in its gentle but precise steering, its brakes — their response is immediate — and its relatively powerful and responsive motor delivering smooth performance. The 52 Mercury hardly bounces on its suspension, and any motion is practically absorbed by the heavily upholstered seats.

For lovers of the Lincoln which some years earlier had launched the visible spare wheel, there was the optional "Continental kit" with spare resting on the trunk lid and extended bumpers. This option was most welcome since it refined the look of the Mercury without overburdening its rear end.

By the way, have you any idea where the name Mercury comes from and when the marque first appeared with Ford? No? Then here it is. It was in 1938 that father and son, Henry and Edsel Ford, decided to create a new marque to compete with the middle-class automobiles of other makers. It was simple to design and build it: the idea was that the new model should basically reflect all the features of the Ford but with somewhat superior fittings

Mercury Turnpike Cruiser with the "Continental Kit", and was Indy Pace Car in 1957. The comprehensive instrumentation included a rev counter

and finish. Edsel headed the design department which produced the first Mercury after a few months of effort. Why Mercury? It went something like this: as was customary at Ford, they made a list of some hundred names, then started to argue. One of the 104 suggestions was Mercury. It was selected, and that was that. What could be simpler?

Right up to 1956 the Mercury marque deliberately ignored the fashion for fins — there was not the slightest rear excrescence, not even the kind of protuberance that had been sported by Cadillac for so long, a sort of blister abandoned at the end of the fender like a slice of cake on the edge of a table. In the meantime, in 1954, Mercury had brought out the Sun Valley featuring a transparent plastic roof. According to its designers, this would enable the occupants to gaze at the wide-open spaces (it was tinted green) and still enjoy air conditioning. A sort of mixture between convertible and sedan. Unfortunately the roof aged quickly; in the sun it soon began to crack up and buyers gradually rejected it. It was also during 1954 that the V8's power was boosted to a feverish 161 hp. After the Monterey and the Sun Valley, Mercury brought out the Montclair in 1955, and the entire range was fitted with a wraparound windshield. Under the hood, the engine put on a few more pounds to give 188 horsepower at the crankshaft.

1957 was to be a fateful year for the Mercury marque. Cruel lines now swept away the flowing style of earlier models; gone was all thought of common sense and reason, things had to be big. Stylists gave free rein to their subconscious fantasies. Bumpers became locomotive buffers surmounted by grimacing grilles. Headlamps were dual beneath sharp "kidney-cutters". The rear quarters were no less crazy: you can almost smell the sulphur, feel the third degree burns. The V-shape lights were a continuation of the waistline tortured to its limits. This madness in metal reached its climax with the Turnpike Cruiser, the violence of whose lines was accentuated by two-tone colour schemes and a sequence of chrome-plated rods and aluminium trim whose effect was nothing short of brutal. Contrary to many other marques who persisted with this outlandish styling up to 1961, Mercury called a halt in 1959. Styles were just as crazy as in 1957 but the lines were more drawn-out, thus lengthening a car of already superhuman proportions.

The creme de la creme, the special treat that you leave till last, was the Turnpike Cruiser convertible. Why? Simply because it was the car that became the official Pace Car for the Indy 500. Hence it was a limited edition of which 1265 were made in California, one model for each of the marque's dealers. The first original feature was its electric roof. Secondly, three "500 miles" motifs were mounted on the fenders at front and the deck at rear. The instrument panel incorporated a rev counter — still unusual for its time — that paired up with a clock, both of which had a rubber vizor. A mini-computer recorded average speed over the road. What else? Oh yes, the seat. This was called Seat-O-Matic, for the driver could adjust it to 49 different positions, and not one more, automatically. Then there was the automatic transmission: speeds were selected by means of push-buttons, after the old manner established by Chrysler. On the mechanical side, the Turnpike was equipped with a small-block of 312 cubic inches developing 290 hp, with which it was credited with a top speed of 110 mph and brutal acceleration.

The Turnpike Cruiser versions returned 17,000 sales in one year — not much. There were two reasons why: first its high price, second its aggressive, irrational styling despite the trend to more Gothic, tormented shapes. They say that once you have got your customers used to a certain staidness of style, they won't let you go over the top.

Next page *The Monterey Coupe also sporting a "Continental Kit". This was the 1953 model*

Mercury

Thunderbird

"Thunderbird, now there's a well-chosen name! A name that exploded onto the consciousness of young America at the time. When it first appeared in 1955 my heart missed a beat, I was totally captivated by its low, balanced lines and its two seats. After the Corvette, America finally came up with its second sports car capable of rivalling the Jaguars and Porsches from Europe."

The speaker here was a mature lady, maybe around sixty; she was sitting on a camp stool, dressed in pink, just ten feet from a magnificent 1956 T-Bird. The car was pink too, just like that lady's dress. On this super-sundrenched Sunday, she sat there, waiting for the judges to come and scrutinize her car. It was a real Californian Sunday, calm and peaceful. A few old car buffs had gathered at this little spot just a few miles from San Francisco to take part in a concours d'elegance, though it was more like a competition for the best condition. Three-quarters of the cars there were in a condition that an average European cannot even begin to suspect — like the T-Bird that belonged to the lady in pink.

She said that her husband had owned a car like it in 1957 and had sold it two years later. A few years ago he had suddenly wanted to own that car again. He bought it for 7000 dollars; it was in good condition but far from being good enough to be seen in a competition like this. So, taking his courage in both hands, he had dismantled the car — completely. The body was taken off the chassis, and engine, gearbox and suspension dropped to the ground. The restoration process took several months: he had to rebuild the mechanics, re-chrome bumpers and windshield surround, and find certain rubber mouldings. Today, the T-Bird looked truly regal, and to get it this way the couple had spent an extra 12,000 dollars, bringing the total cost of their dream car up to 20,000.

The lady dressed in pink, sitting on her folding chair, got first prize out of all the assembled T-Birds.

The first thing that strikes you when you look at a 55 or 56 T-Bird is the regularity of its lines, the refinement of its front end which is only very slightly emphasized by the simple grille. The bumpers are lightweight, and the rear quarters are as sensible as the front. There are those of course, for whom any T-Bird (and for that matter any Corvette) is wonderful, but I have to confess that, to me at least, my favourite is the 1956 model with the outside spare. Despite its sporty and aggressive air, the car nevertheless retains a certain delicacy of form, a definite gentleness that never fails to bring a lump to my throat.

The T-Bird's restrained looks are all the more surprising when you think that 1955 was the year of fin madness, massive, tortured grilles, two-tone colour schemes — sometimes violently clashing — and side mouldings as fat as a butcher's hand. The T-Bird thankfully escaped this treatment, at least up to 1958 that is, when a radical transformation made it unbelievably ugly and gave it four seats. This pretty roadster, introduced in 1955, was to retain its basic characteristics throughout its life, i.e. three years. During this time nothing major was changed except the engine. From 1958 onwards — well, wait and see.

The traditional origins of the T-Bird have something odd about them. The story goes that the idea for a two-seater came from Ford's general manager, Lewis Crusoe, when he visited an automobile salon at Paris and discovered European sports cars like Jaguar, Mercedes and Ferrari. On his return to the States he expressed his surprise that Ford had nothing of the kind to offer. The story is curious enough — was Crusoe so ignorant? Was he completely unaware of the existence of these

sports cars? If so, he must also have been unaware of the Corvette which had been around for two years!

We find no answer to these questions; let's just say that there are some nice stories that are repeated until they become history. Anyway, the fact was that Crusoe's surprise on his return home caused panic among Ford executives — how was it that a company as powerful as Ford had no two-seater sports car in its line-up? What an oversight! What an error!

The oversight and the error were quickly made good. The car came out in 1955 at the competitive price of 2944 dollars, just 10 dollars more that the Corvette of the same year. The T-Bird's price was of course geared to the Vette's so that the Ford would at least have a fair chance.

In fact, it's success was blinding. With a burst that was as mystifying as it was marvellous, the newcomer achieved 15,000 sales against the Corvette's 700; the year before, the Vette was still selling around 3200 units, which means that, right from its entry upon the scene, the T-Bird stole a hefty chunk of the Vette's public.

A truly amazing feat. Ford executives could not believe their ears. But would it last? Wasn't it all just a flash in the pan? The figures prove that it wasn't. The year after, the T-Bird was adorned with its outside spare, and sales soared to 18,500, while the Corvette got no more than 6339. This trend increased: in 1958 53,000 T-Birds were sold against the Corvette's meagre 9000. 1960 was the zenith of this success: 87,000 Thunderbirds left the assembly lines against just 12,500 unhappy Corvettes.

The statistics are significant. They show that the car's aesthetic qualities were without equal. Likewise its road performance. The name "Thunderbird", chosen because it symbolizes power and prosperity (?), fulfilled its promise.

The Thunderbird had no trouble standing comparisons with other racers. Beneath the hood, Ford dug out its old 272 cubic inch and turned it into 292 developing 202 horsepower; wheelbase was a mini 102 inches. The transmission was manual after the fashion of European sports cars. 1956 brought no change to styling except for the spare wheel which

One of the great Ford successes, the Thunderbird far outclassed its rival Corvette from its appearance in 1955. Shown here is the 1956 model outside spare and porthole hardtop. Next page *The same model photographed in Paris. It had pure lines and an elegant dashboard*

Thunderbird

The T-Bird's functional instrumentation, with central speedometer, tachometer for 5000 rpm at left, and clock at right

added elegance to its clean, pure lines. There was now a choice between two engines, the 292 cu. in. giving 202 hp through a manual box, or the 312 cubic inch (215 hp) fitted to cars with manual transmission plus overdrive or with the Fordomatic auto transmission for which the engine likewise developed 215 hp. Unlike the Corvette, the instrument panel on the T-Bird was of superb simplicity: just a plain dash with a single big dial right in the driver's line of vision and the customary instruments. In 1957 the T-Bird was still a two-seater. However the body was substantially facelifted, which did nothing for it. The grille was now underscored by a heavy bumper, while the rear fenders began to sprout little fins. The hub caps were redesigned and the outside spare which had given the car so much chic was tossed back inside the trunk. Engines were the same; only the 312 grew in power with a 245 hp version. The car retailed at 3408 dollars against the Corvette's 3465. And that was the end of the pretty little two-seater coupe, just three years after its first appearance. For

months, the styling department had been looking at a 4-seat T-Bird, much in demand by customers, as various market surveys proved. In 1958, the press discovered the new-look Thunderbird. In truth, the press did not exactly rave about the new car, though the four-seat formula was widely applauded. It was just that the car had lost all its charm and finesse. The grille was integral in the bumper to form a kind of huge fishmouth. The heavy side panels were laden with mouldings and rear fenders ended in a rather low fin. What was striking, in fact, was the car's overall impression of weight and heaviness throughout. Still, it was warmly received by the public who bought 53,000 in the space of one year as compared with 20,000 the year before for the 2-seater. Ford's gamble had paid off. The true sports car such as Europe conceives it was just not made for the American masses, and each succeeding year proved that a four-seater with modern styling is more profitable than an engine hidden in front of a couple of skimpy seats.
The car's general look was retained

Thunderbird

until 1960 with the exception of a few details. It was still the big coupe, 113 inch wheelbase, propelled by a 352 cubic inch engine giving 300 hp in the standard version (price was 4222 dollars). For speed merchants there was a more powerful engine. This was the power pack fitted to the Lincoln Continental, its 430 cubic inches giving out 350 hp at 4600 rpm. The car came as a coupe or convertible. The hardtops were most in demand and sold seven times the number of convertibles, proving, if proof were still needed, that Americans at that time preferred luxury and comfort to the joys of the open sports car with its breezes.

The Thunderbird was totally reviewed and restyled every three years. In 1961 the new model's front end was curiously reminiscent of the Lincoln Continental, hardly surprising since both cars were styled by the same man. Side panels were flat and very clean. The panoramic windshield had disappeared, while the simpler rear quarters were enhanced by two enormous red lights. Available as a hardtop or convertible as always (no point in changing habits) greater attention was paid to the chassis. Although the initial idea was to build a front-wheel drive, propulsion stayed traditional. Engineers instead concentrated on precision construction and the strict quality control of each individual component, also on eliminating noise caused by tyres, engine and body. The new T-Bird's engine, unique to 1961, was the 390 cubic inch V8 of 300 horsepower. In 1962 there were two engines, the eternal, reliable 390, plus the same again but this time wrapped in a package boosting the trip to 340 hp. Interior finish was lovingly designed, and in a car that featured luxury before performance, everything was electric. There was even an ingenious system that allowed the steering wheel to be swivelled to the right to make installation easier for the driver. For me, one of the most beautiful T-Birds is still the Sports Roadster that was produced in 62 and 63.

Full rear view of the T-Bird

This was a 4-seater convertible simply transformed into a 2-seater. The man responsible for this idea was Lee Iacocca, a Ford director, who was being lobbied by some dealers to bring out a two-seat roadster. A stylist was duly set to work, but Iacocca never really believed in the success of this enterprise. For him, the day of the lean convertible had gone. It had met a profitable public demand for a while in the Fifties, but people's taste and attitudes had changed. So rather than wasting time — and money — on a totally new project, he made a tonneau cover to hide the T-Bird's rear seats. The result was magnificent: the shortened cabin, now terminating in a pair of head restraints, gave the car a rakish look. The new 2-seater T-Bird was a noble beast, elegant, thoroughbred and fine as a steel blade. But the transformation was excessively costly: 650 dollars were added on to the already considerable price of 5439 dollars for the T-Bird proper.

It was an idea built on the shifting sands of fashion, as Lee Iacocca had suspected. Despite the T-Bird's quality styling, the 2-seater did not sell. In 1962 1427 vehicles were produced, just 455 in 1963. A total failure. Which is a pity because the Sports Roadster was to be the last of the "great" Thunderbirds.

Thunderbird

The T-Bird Sports
Roadster was produced in
1962 and 1963. It was in
fact a four-seater
drophead converted to a
two-seater with the aid of
a polyester tonneau cover.
It was priced at 5500
dollars at the time.
Opposite The facelifted,
dual headlight 64 T-Bird.
The steering wheel slewed
sideways to afford ease of
access to driver

Thunderbird

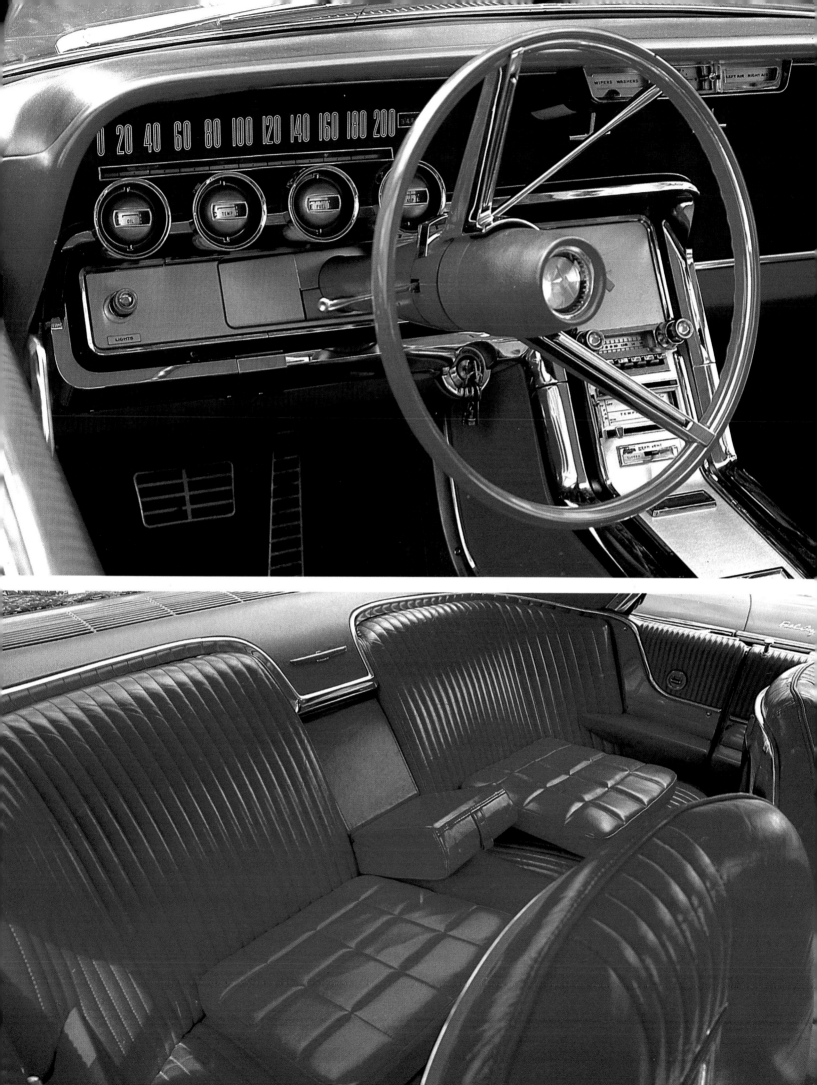

Mustang

The Mustang was really something! A total success in Europe as much as the States, something quite unheard of. The first models appeared in 1964 but the idea went back to 1961, when Lee Iacocca, engineer and sales director at Ford at the time, realized that there was a strong latent demand for a small two-seater sports car of the kind that had disappeared at the close of the Fifties with the Thunderbird. The car also had to be popularly priced.

A number of prototypes were designed and it was decided that the car would have four seats but that its styling would be very sporty. And so the Mustang was designed along the criteria of long hood, low lines and a relatively short tail. The car was indeed compact, almost squat, but Iacocca's trick was to offer a multitude of options, both in terms of power plant and finish. Its commercial success was immediate, the Mustang's sales figures were just unreal. Its record was, and still is, unbeaten. All America desired the car, men, women and teenagers with brand new driving licences. There were three models, the GT 2 + 2 fastback, the convertible and the two-door hardtop. In the initial years the convertible's success was astounding, with sales topping 100,000 a year! Starting from the principle that the Mustang had to be the archetypal popular car, its basic equipment was painfully sparse, with an engine borrowed from the wretched Falcon, one on the first compact cars, its capacity a miserly 170 cubic inches. This cast-iron straight six was enormous in weight and turned out a pathetic 101 hp. I say pathetic because the Mustang was supposed to be a sports car, and its 101 horsepower were not exactly going to propel it at incredible speeds.

As it turned out however, the policy of a beautiful body hiding a little engine for those of modest means was one of the best ideas Ford's bosses ever had. Now everyone could make his sports car dream come true, even if performance was not unlike a Citroën 2 CV. The idea was repeated some years later by Ford of Europe with the Capri at first with a micromotor in a pretty shell. Thank God for those options! During the first few months of production, at least, the buyer could choose a small-block V8 260 cubic inch engine developing a still somewhat miserly 164 hp. Subsequently, the 170 cu.in. was increased to 200 to give 120 hp, while the 260 cu.in. was superseded by the famous 289 cu.in. V8 developing 200 hp with its small carburettor and 270 hp with a four-barrel. The 200 hp version made the trip across the Atlantic and settled in Europe in large numbers.

It was a marvellous engine, warmly responsive, especially when coupled to a manual four-speed box that made it easy to push the needle up to 125 mph. At this speed the engine was happy, free from strain there was no overheating, in traffic jams too. The chief quality of the 289 cubic inch was its sturdiness. It was ready for anything, as solid as granite, at home at any revs. The only thing that Mustang owners complained of was the steering which, while direct, lacked precision. Even when sold fully loaded the car's finish was little more than random, and it put the car exactly where its designers wanted it to be, hardly at the top of the Ford tree. It is worth remembering that the basic price in 1965 was just 2368 dollars for the six cylinder Mustang and 2722 for the V8 model. In 1966 the straight six disappeared and prices where kept down: 2416 dollars for the 200 hp, while the 270 hp version came in at 2653 dollars. As the years passed, the Mustang forsook its agreeable, value-for-money image and saw its power grow incessantly. In 1967 for instance Ford proposed a 390 cubic inch big-block developing 320 hp, while one year later Ford brought out its biggest engine, a 427 cu.in. giving a monster 400 horsepower. You will recall that American engine ratings were calculated according to SAE standards, which meant that the power was that measured at the crankshaft without ancilleries taking off any energy; fan, assorted servos, air-conditioning and above all the gearbox. With all these deducted, final power at the road wheels was some 25 to 40 per cent below the published rating.

By offering a veritable plethora of options Ford hoped to get through to a broad clientele. Apart from the engines there were transmissions, three and four speed manual boxes and automatics, dashboard detail, rev counter, central console, electric windows, bucket seats. There was even a "package" for 170 dollars extra comprising front disc brakes, a super-comprehensive instrument panel and special decor.

By now we are well out of the Fifties, but the Mustang was a logical consequence of that decade. After the razor-sharp fins of 1959, stylists returned to lines that were clean, grilles that were sober and styles that were distinctly European in flavour. The Mustang's classicism makes it a model of automotive beauty. I'd rather not mention its successor, the Mustang II, a real little horror on wheels.

The Mustang was born in 1965. This 2+2 Fastback Coupe was the most popular version

Pictures of the 65
Mustang cabriolet.
Opposite *The notchback
hardtop. A most
interesting engine of 289
cubic inches under the
hood*

Mustang

**GENERAL
MOTORS**

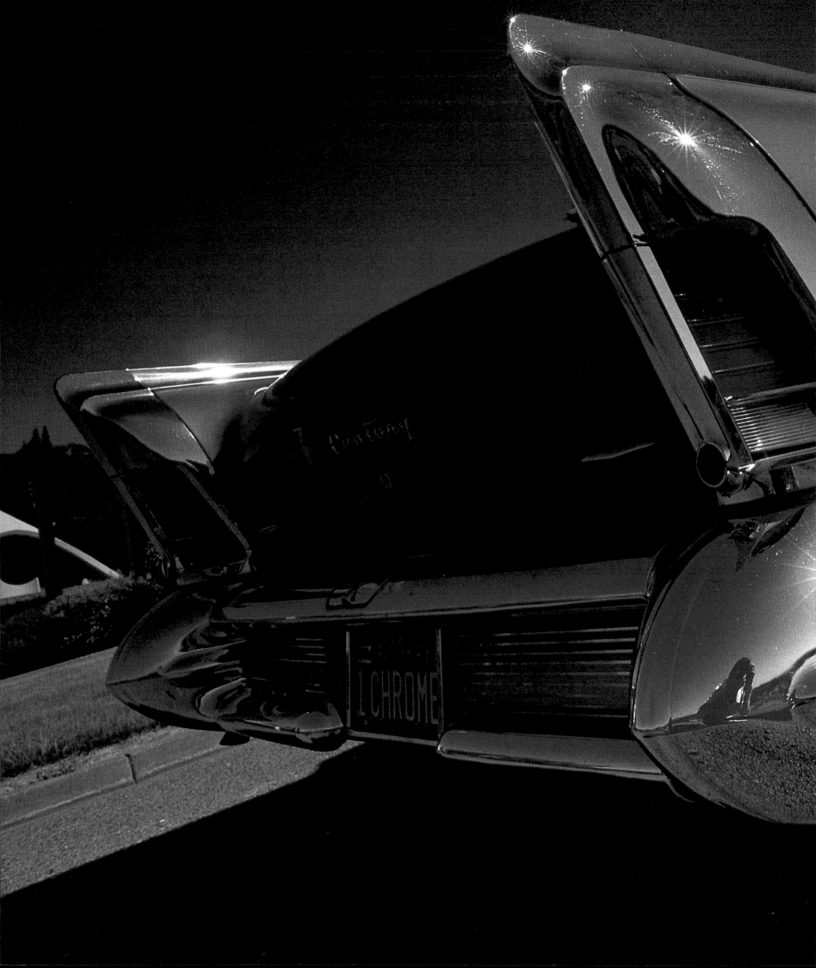

Buick

David Buick was an inventor and producer of industrial products, including bath tubs! Unfortunately, although a fount of ideas, this upstanding man was totally ignorant of accountancy.

The first casualty of this ignorance was his plumbing business, and the second was his automobile business, which was taken over by General Motors in 1903. The head of GM was a certain Crapo Durant, a man with an instinctive business sense. It was his intention to turn Buick into the best car for the middle classes, just behind Cadillac and Lincoln, the acknowledged upper class automobiles. In this he succeeded.

The production of Buicks began modestly in 1904, when only 37 cars were produced. By 1905 750 models were turned out, placing the new make in ninth place in the league table of American automobile production.

As for the engine, this was not yet the V8 or even the V16, and still less the future V12 of Cadillac. It was only in 1931 that this car was fitted with a new engine in the form of a straight eight which remained in production for 22 years, a true demonstration of the longevity. These were quiet years for Buick and little of note was to happen until the Fifties. However, the already old-fashioned engine had by then been linked to a semi-synchronized gearbox, the Synchromesh, making an exceptionally fine unit. The straight eight was as silent and powerful as a vacuum cleaner!

During the Thirties Buick produced the Century. This model first appeared in 1936 and was the first "middle-class" car to have a maximum speed of more than 100 mph. Later, the Limited, Roadmaster and Century were equipped with a new engine; this was still the usual straight eight, but with a capacity of 320 cubic inches and 120 hp. The Buick Special, the small Buick, however, was only given a capacity of 233 cubic inches, developing 93 horse power. At the end of the Thirties two important innovations were introduced which were to have lasting significance : from 1937 the four wheels were equipped with coil spring suspension, which increased the road-holding of the car; in the same year appeared the four-gear semi-automatic Self-Shifter...

As far as bodywork was concerned, Buick did not take any risks, unlike the Chrysler Airflow which, in 1934, assumed an aerodynamic body. Buick maintained a solid, conservative image and followed fashion with moderation. However, all Buick bodies had one common characteristic: size. They always looked large and impressive.

Buick did follow the fashion for the "fastback" models which were produced by others at the end of the Forties. These were elegant four-seaters which had two doors and a back which continued the line of the roof in a gentle slope. In this category were the Super of 1946 and the Riviera of 1949. In 1948 a major mechanical innovation was introduced in the Roadmaster, which was the principal model. The huge straight eight, which still had a capacity of 320 cubic inches and developed 114 hp at 3600 revs, was linked to an auto transmission, the Dynaflow. By this time automobiles had developed into sheetmetal monsters, whose force and power were best expressed in massively exaggerated grilles composed essentially of great steel teeth. The most famous and successful expression of this style was the model of 1950.

The most prestigious automobile produced by GM was, of course, the Cadillac. The Buick was, however, not very far behind. For years Cadillac had produced models with V8 engines, while Buicks had always been equipped with straight sixes or eights — a fact which does seem a little strange. This difference finally disappeared in 1953, when a V8 was

Buick

finally introduced on their fiftieth anniversary. We should not at this point forget the beautiful Riviera Roadmaster of 1949, the first car to be provided with a hardtop, with its famous "portholes" on the front fenders. The luxury model in the Buick range was the Skylark which was built on the chassis of the Roadmaster. This was an extremely elegant car, in spite of its massive lines; these were relieved by the addition of spoked wheels and wooden trimming in the form of a shallow V at door level. The launch of the model was attended by the highest hopes and the heads of the company forecast spectacular sales. In fact, just the opposite happened. In spite of being equipped with a 322 engine which developed 188 hp thanks to its four-barrel, this model only had sales of 1690. The principle cause of its failure was the 5000 dollars price.

Less prestigious, but just as big, were the Super and the Roadmaster. The Super's 322 engine was slightly less powerful because of its two barres carburettor and developed 164 hp with normal transmission and 170 when equipped with the Dynaflow. The Roadmaster developed 188 hp. The small model, the Special, still retained the straight eight with a capacity of 263 cubic inches, developing a miserable 130 hp.

From 1954 Buick began to follow the style of Cadillac and to introduce models with fins which reinforced the impression of calculated aggression. The trunk of the Century — which was equipped with a 200 hp V8 engine — was embellished with two chromed protuberances. The grilles were also styled like those of the Cadillacs with "shell" fenders (Century 1955).

The crazy embellishment of models with useless metal reached its peak in 1958, a fateful year. The front of the vehicle has taken on the heavy lines of a drawbridge, while the straight radiator grille has been decorated with dozens of small shiny squares; the top, now large enough the house a street fair, is as high as a 16th century cupboard. The pano-

The impressive form of a Buick Roadmaster of 1949 posing in front of the Queen Mary. Next page *Ten years later — the Electra 225 cabriolet with sharp edges everywhere*

ramic windshields is still there, matched by the rear window, which is of similar size and style. The fenders are veritable poems in chrome, a symphony of reflection.

The Century Roadmaster and the new Limited, launched in 1958, had rear ends which were even crazier than the rest. On each side of the car the fenders were swept up into a kind of ball which looked as though it had been intended for use in demolition work. The headlights reflected the style of the fenders and were so heavily mounted in chrome that they almost appeared to have been inserted in medieval suits of armour. These Buicks were either loved or left. Either their owners rapidly got fed up with them or they turned themselves into contortionists to polish each centimetre. The flanks of these bulldozer-cars were thus made to shine in reflection of their power. But what are we to think of this fashion?

Not a lot, perhaps. Its admirers, and there are many in the States, take good care of these brilliant masses of metal so that their bodies gleam as though in the glare of a thousand suns. Buick called this fashion "The Air Born B-58 Buick". This says it all: the power of the airplane, linked to its destructive capacity.

The following year the fashion continued its course, taking the opportunity to drop the one element which made these cars so brutal — the chromework. The chrome of the fenders, radiator grilles and wings miraculously disappeared. However, as can be seen in the Buick Electra 225, the fins were extended even further. For me, however, this style was one of the most perfect expressions of what was understood by the "Fifties" in America.

Buick

Cadillac

The history of the Cadillac is a true epic of the automobile world. The story begins in 1902 and continues to our own times with all the power and pride of a history of constant success

At the beginning of the century, the high-class car which most successfully combined versatility, finish and classical beauty was the Packard. Its position at the top was never contested. Later, a similar position came to be held by the Pierce-Arrow, then, at the beginning of the Twenties, by the incredible Duesenberg. During the first three decades of the century, low-class cars were powered by four-cylinder engines, middle-class cars by six cylinders, and the upper crust by straight eights.

The advent of Cadillac into this settled world upset all the dearly held mechanical principles of the men who ran it. First came the launch in 1915 (in 1915!) of a magnificent V8 which, though powerful, took up a minimum of space under the hood. Then in 1928, Cadillac — now the premier make of GM — unveiled a second innovation, which was entirely unexpected. This was the Syncromesch transmission which, for the first time, incorporated synchronized second and third gears, making the whole process of gear-changing quite easy. This was a real revolution in an industry which concerned itself very much with the development of solid and luxurious products, but had little wish to introduce mechanical change.

The arrival of Cadillac was to change all that. And the technical ingenuity did not come to a halt there. In January 1930 Cadillac produced yet another trick it had been holding up its sleeve at the New York automobile show. This was an absolutely monumental engine: its first V6. Its power was unbelievable, with its 452 cubic inches and 165 hp,

all going with marvellous smoothness. Almost 2500 cars equipped with this engine were sold in a single year. Unfortunately, the economic crisis was to bring its commercial progress to an end. One year later, Cadillac brought out its V12, which was of such technical excellence, that the company leapt years ahead of its rivals. It is important to remember, too, that Cadillac did not only introduce new engines, but also improved the existing ones. The V16 of 1930 was, then, substantially remodelled in 1938. The two banks of cylinders formed an angle of 135 degrees, treated as two joined V8s. This engine was more powerful than the first V16, developing 185 hp at 3600 rpm. And what, then, of the Fifties. If the Cadillac has become one of the most prestigious cars of the past three decades then it is because of the developments so lightly described above. It is absolutely essential to trace the development of this automobile in relation to its other American rivals over a long period. During that time, its rivals disappeared one after another. Not one of them was able to withstand the competition, either because of lack of investment, good management or because of a the lack of competetive prices. Every one of them at some point committed a cardinal error from which they were unable to recover.

A few other facts are worth remembering in an examination of the pre-eminence of Cadillac. From 1940, the V12s end the V16s were abandoned. It had been discovered that a good V8 could return to same performance as an expensive V16, which was difficult to maintain and twice as heavy. At the beginning of the war, all Cadillacs were powered by a large V8 of 346 cubic inches, developing 150 hp. This may not seem especially powerful, but it must be remembered that cars were getting lighter. Then there was the optional automatic Hydromatic gearbox, as well as air-conditioning. In 1940, Cadillac sold more than 66,000 cars, a record which was to stand until 1949. We are slowly getting closer to the

Fifties. But before then another technical innovation was to give another lease of life to the V8 Cadillac. Strictly speaking, there were two innovations, the second being in style — a style which was to influence all American car manufacturers for 20 years and was only to die in the Sixties from its own excesses.

It was in 1949 that Cadillac took the automobile world totally by surprise. The occasion was the launch of its new overhead valve V8. The camshaft was positioned centrally and the valves operated by hydraulic push-rods. This was a true modern engine. It was more powerful than the old V8 of 346 cubic inches, smaller (331 cubic inches) and lighter. With the exception of the powerful V16s of the pre-war years, this was the most powerful ever Cadillac engine. It developped 160 hp, giving a speed of more than 100 mph.

The second innovation of the year was the change in styling. The new Cadillac bodywork was quite revolutionary and was due to a certain Harley Earl. In our first chapter we saw how this brillant man, after designing the P.38 warplane with its enormous tail, applied a design with protruding surfaces to the bodywork styling of 1947. Admittedly these were only modest protrusions, but gradually they developed into the crazy flights of fancy of 1956, reaching their peak in 1959.

At the beginning of the Fifties a type 62 Town Coupe cost 3843 dollars. The following year a model 62 Sedan cost 3684 dollars, or little less than double the price of a Buick of the same capacity. This may have seemed expensive, but there was no doubt about Cadillac quality. Every engine part was assembled under careful control and the eventual completion was carried in conditions far superior to any other. There were other manufacturers, such as Imperial, which took as much care, but their prices were appreciably higher than those of Cadillac. Only Packard could claim to be in direct competition until the beginning of the Fifties, with prices which were wholly competitive. The only problem with that declining make was that the product was out-of-date. Mechanically, there was no comparison between a Packard and a Cadillac, which now possessed a modern engine, an automatic four speed gearbox an infinite variety of options, electric windows, etc. In addition, and this is very important in a country where everyone wants something different, the variety of Cadillac models was condiderable. Until 1951, the buyer could choose between the "61", "62", "60.S" or "75" series, which included berlines, cabriolets, coupes and limousines.

Just for the record, we should note that the "61" models had a wheelbase of 122 inches, while the "62" models had one of 126. The luxury models of the "60.S" series had a 130-inch chassis, while the wheelbase of "75" limousines was 146 inches. The least expensive models were those of the small wheelbase series "61", which were 350 dollars less than the "62" series, the most popular. The "61" series ceased production in 1952.

Aesthetically speaking, Cadillac had heavy, rounded lines, with wooden trimming placed quite high. Apart from the two slim fins which revolutionised the automobile world, the remainder of the body was fairly classical. The radiator grille was piece of chrome which was extended into the thick bumpers.

For four years, from 1950 to 1953, Cadillac kept the same bodywork. The grille and bumpers were subject to small changes and, from 1952, the exhausts came out of the rear bumpers. But these changes were of no consequence. The real revolution was to come in 1953.

First came a new V8, developing 210 hp at 4150 revs/min. And then came the birth of the Eldorado, a high-specification, luxury automobile. The Eldo was only manufactured in its cabriolet form and its production was limited because of its high price 7750 dollars (532 models). The Eldorado reflected the lines of the other

Cadillac

111

The Cadillac of 1949 had already been given small fins behind. Under the hood, the new cubic-inch V8 with overhead valves developed 160 hp. Right, top *A 1956 Cadillac cabriolet with a 285 hp engine.* Bottom *The Eldorado Biarritz cabriolet with a soft top in polyester and alloy wheels: its price was 6500 dollars*

Cadillac

models, but was also given a panoramic windshield. This type of windshield became the great innovation for all the models of 1954, which also had their grilles restyled and refined. That year also saw the engine increased in power to 230 hp. Although standard models of the range kept their styling until 1956, the Eldorado was given a completely new body in 1955 which was wholly individual. The fins in the form of small balls, which we all know so well, were replaced by sharp, emphatic spurs. This car had light alloy instead of spoked wheels. Among the wealth of accessories and gadgets, there was an electronic eye which enabled the automatic switching from dipped to main beam and vice-versa. This novelty was really only icing on the cake, since the system was not particularly reliable. It only needed a number of light sources of different strengths to be positioned close to each other for the whole system to become completely erratic. Many of the owners of cars thus equipped had the photo-electric eye suppressed altogether.

In 1957 a degree of madness seems to have overtaken Cadillac. Completely redesigned, all the models were equipped with the panoramic windshield, a heavily embellished front and fins as sharp as cacti. The engine developed 300 hp, with an option for all models of 325. Thanks to the extensive range of models and the quality of the finished product, Cadillac became the most widely sold American luxury car. In 1950 the Cadillac division of GM sold more than 100,000 cars. By 1955 this figure had become 150,000, reaching a peak of 200,000 in 1960. It could have been thought that the size of bodies and the wild lines of the fins would have put off the more traditional clients. But such was not the case: when Lincoln brought out a very classical four-door berline in 1961, Cadillac sales were in no way affected.

This wildness of style in the cars is perfectly represented by the Eldorado range of 1957. Always a year ahead of other cars, Cadillac introduced an Eldorado cabriolet called the Biarritz, a hardtop coupe called the Seville, and the famous Brougham, a columnless four-door with an aluminium roof. The Eldorado Biarritz and Seville had the usual Cadillac hood, but the back was totally different. The coupe and the cabriolet had optional wings or fins, which were separete from the main fender. This made them look more like flappers than fishtails. And all this was surrounded by a mass of chrome, rounded and brightly shining, which took America by storm. Firstly, because revolutionary styling is often provocative and then because the price of the cabriolet and the hardtop coupe was a staggering 7286 dollars, which only the minority could pay.

At the same time, 1957, that these Cadillacs cost more than, 7000 dollars, the big Buick was only 4483 dollars, and the top Chevrolet a mere 3500 dollars. Even a Chrysler would hardly have cost 5000 collars. There was, of course, the Lincoln Continental, launched in 1956, which was on the market at 10,000 dollars. All the same, what was so special about the Cadillac that it cost almost 7300 dollars?

The answer is, almost everything. Its engine was powerful and odourless. It had a four-speed automatic in which the passage from one gear to the next was imperceptible, even in reverse. The interior was covered in hand-stitched leather. There were windows, deflectors, seat, trunk opening, hood, clock, and many other luxury items — all electric. The Eldo was a monster which could be seen ten miles away. There was no chance of mistaking that scowling, threatening rear, which finished off this automobile marvel, 6.5 feet wide and 18.3 feet in length.

What, then, was the Eldorado like to drive? The sensation of driving the car must have been extraordinary, especially if you wanted to be carried along at 125 mph, the tyres making a terrific noise on the asphalt. It was, in any case, a car

Cadillac

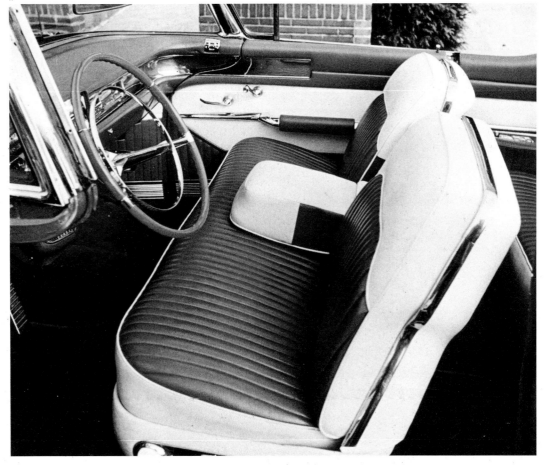

An Eldorado Biarritz of 1957 equipped with a Hydra-Matic gearbox and every imaginable electrical instrument. Next page The dashboard of the Eldo Biarritz of 1957; above and to the left of the steering wheel can be seen the little red box housing the Autronic Eye (automatic headlamp adjustment)

Cadillac

After the supreme folly of the quite terrifying fins of the 1959 Cadillac, the 1960 model looked quite sober: The grille remained very aggressive, while the rear lights looked like electric razors. The fins were still very sharp

Cadillac

which held the road well. There was power-assisted steering and an immense steering wheel which could be guided with two fingers. At the same time, however, the steering tended to be too imprecise. The drum brakes were power-assisted so that the car could be slowed down with great smoothness. They could not, however, be used violently, since they very rapidly lost power. After three energetic applications to stop the 2.3. tons, the right foot would suddenly meet no more resistance. Even the famous road-holding qualities had their limitations. There was nothing to complain about in wide bends. The bodywork would follow the line of road comfortably, the front slightly understeered and the back remaining nicely in place. In rain, however, it was a different story, and a lot of caution had to be exercised in applying the accelerator.

In tight bends the car would obstinately refuse to steer properly. And if the driver continued to apply the brakes, the bloated hood would simply continue its forward trajectory, even if the front wheels were locked over. It was then that the driver would realize who was the master of whom. This, then, was the Eldorado. It needed a gentleness of touch, no sudden movements, and perhaps, from time to time, a short burst of speed, just to appreciate how lively those eight pistons could be. Any wildness in this automobile would have been in bad taste.

For a European, used to driving cars which hold the road and which can brake, such a vehicle would be inconceivable. But we have to remember that we are talking about If 7300 dollars was already a high price, it was nothing beside the 13,074 dollars for an Eldo Brougham. Very few were made of this, the most expensive car available in 1957. It was introduced by General Motors specifically to compete with the Lincoln Continental Mark II. The unique features of the Brougham included pneumatic suspension, a dropped roof, a glove compartment which gave off an odour of perfume (Arpege) and a front different to all the other Cadillacs. This high luxury car was still produced in the States in 1958, but in 1959 and 1960 the Italian Pinin Farina was commissioned to oversee the hand assembly. From this can be concluded that the quality was no longer the same, whatever may have been expected, especially since the price remained the same as in 1958. Ninety-nine models were sold in 1959 and 101 in 1960. Production of this car ended there, just at the end of the Fifties, as if to mark clearly the generation for which it had been intended.

The remainder of the Cadillac range of 1958 was nothing special. The cars had the same fins as the Eldorado of the preceding year, while the engine had become a 310 hp. Mechanically, the Cadillacs remained what they had been the year before, with the same faults and qualities. However, the design of the front was changed. From 1950 to 1956 the hoods had been heavily rounded; each individual form was rounded in some way. This style was somewhat modified in 1957, to disappear altogether in 1958. The hood was now flat, falling directly to join the radiator grille. This grille was rectangular and formed a single unit with the bumper, thus foretelling the shapes of 1959, which were to be the apotheosis of the style.

Whether this was the apotheosis of genius or of bad taste is a matter for argument. The style had its violent critics who were just as vehement in their opinions as the ardent supporters of the style, even though some of these may have been less than public in their support. There is, however, a lesson in the Cadillac of 1959, with its double grille, its double bumper and its fins which were its most exciting feature. This was the apogee of wild car design at its most successful. The 59 Cadillacs, far from being rejected by the public, were enthusiastically welcomed. The standard engine was a 325 hp, with an optional 345 hp.

But anyone who did not buy the 345 hp version did not really deserve to own this terrible and frightening automobile. The fenders were swept back from the bumper to end in the extraordinary unit which housed the double red rear lights which could light up the whole horizon. The design office of the company must have lost all sense of proportion to have dared to have offered such an example of stylistic exaggeration. But the time had to be ready for it. The Cadillac of 1959 is the archetype of uselessness, of the anti-functional. The false grille behind echoes the grille in front; the masses of chrome dazzle the eyes; the expanses of sheet metal seem limitless; the purely decorative function of the forms is of a time which we are unlikely to see again. Only wealthy civilizations can indulge themselves in such "grandeur and decadence".

Next page *The evolution of rear wings.* Top left *The Fleetwood 60-S series;* Bottom *A 1960 cabriolet.* Right *The summit of daring and cruelty, the Cadillac of 1956*

Cadillac

Chevrolet

At the beginning of this century nothing could have been further from the minds of the Swiss Chevrolet brothers, than that their names were to become famous in the automobile industry. Once in America, they began work in the steel industry, eventually manufacturing car components. The obvious conclusion was then reached by the family, that they would launch into the business of making cars, just like Henry Ford.

Like Henry Ford, too, it was decided that the company should make cars in large quantities, so that the initial investment could be amortized as swiftly as possible. The obvious course, then, seemed to be to produce a small, good-quality car at a competitive price.

The Model T Ford was in production from 1908 to 1927, and was replaced in the December of that year by the new Model A. In 1929, Chevrolet made its bid to replace Ford in the popular market, bringing out a very competitive automobile which was described in the accompanying publicity as "six cylinders for the price of four". Although this was a very weighty argument in its favour, the new six cylinder was, unfortunately, not very powerful and only developed 50 hp at 2600 rpm. But the public still seemed to like the make and, by 1931, there were no less than twelve models in the Chevrolet range. In addition to the traditional berlines, the range included an attractive Landau Phaeton and a Sport Roadster, but these two models hardly filled the order books.

The most popular model of the Thirties was the two-door Coach, of which 165,000 models were in the Master series and 70,000 in the Standard series.

It was in that year, 1934, that Chevrolet began to improve their models significantly. The improvements were not especially dramatic, but since Chevrolet was not notable for its advances, they were well worth taking notice of. The main improvement was the introduction of the Knee-Action system, which was in fact no more than the front independent suspension, which replaced the traditional rigid axle. The power of the engine was also increased to 80 hp, which was supposed to give the car a top speed of 80 mph, although that figure seems to have been optimistic.

In short, then, that was the revolution which the Chevrolet brothers brought to the automobile world in the Thirties. Not a particularly glamorous revolution, admittedly; there was no sign of a V8 or automatic gearbox or any other exceptional improvement.

The styling of the Chevrolet was also very ordinary. The models followed the dominant fashion and, at the end of the period, the bodywork finally gave way to streamlining, but without going too far. It was only in 1941 that the Chevrolet engineers finally dared to make a car which did not contain a single piece of wood. This model also saw the introduction of the Victory Six which retained the previous capacity of 216.5 cubic inches, but now developed 90 hp at 3300 rpm.

These improvements, though small, did make for good cars, and the Chevrolets sold well. In 1941, for example, the Town Sedan model sold 228,000, a record, followed by 219,000 of the Master De Luxe, 156,000 of the Special De Luxe, not to mention 80,000 Master De Luxe coupes. Although there was nothing of great technical interest which were made essentially for hard use by the lower middle classes. But America was suitably impressed.

After the war, the sales figures plunged. In 1945 Ford crashed to 37,800 cars, while Chevrolet could not do better than 25,000. Chrysler and Nash could only manage 6000, while the rest were negligible. This

phase, which was a direct result of the Second World War, was only of short duration. By 1947 sales figures had started to climb steeply again and GM took up the challenge again, producing 1,400,000 units against Chrysler's 780,000 and Ford's 755,000. The sales war was particularly hard among the three "greats" and it only needed one bad model in this immense production for a company to lose face.

The coming of the Fifties found Chevrolet still with the reputation of producing lower class cars. One of the reasons for this reputation was that no Chevrolet, unlike the Fords, had ever been equipped with a V8. Automatic transmission, the Power-Glide, had only just been introduced and the so-called luxury models were still very far from having the quality and finish of their direct rivals.

From 1946 ot 1950, however, one model did enjoy a certain amount of success. This was the "fastback", and the Chevrolet version was called the Fleetline. The fashion lasted until 1952, by which year production had declined to 37,000. This was a pity, because this model was certainly the most original Chevrolet of the For-

ties and early Fifties. From 1950 to 1952 Chevrolet still retained the image of being a manufacturer of modest cars at low prices. Apart from the two-speed automatic transmission introduced in 1950, the rest of the mechanical specification changed little. The engine was still the old straight six, the "stove bolt six", developing its 92 hp and 3400 rpm. The models equipped with the Power-Glide did, however, have more: 105 hp at 3600 revs.

We should not forget the undoubted virtues of the Chevrolets of the time. Although they retained their rather poverty-stricken image, they were sold at unbeatable prices, which eventually allowed them to overtake their rivals in sales volume. In 1950, Chevrolet introduced a coupe which was an immediate success. That year it sold 76,000 units and the following year 103,000, over-taking similar sired Fords and Plymouths. In 1952, Chevrolet did introduce a number of improvements, though none was especially revolutionary. There was a new steering wheel, a choice of 26 colours, more absorbant dampers making driving smoother and giving better road holding. The new models

All the Chevrolet bodies were redesigned in 1953. This coupe has been finally equipped with a one-piece windshield. Next page A very fine Bel Air coupe of 1955 which was powered either by a 136 or 180 hp engine

Chevrolet

*A very fine two-door
Nomad brake of 1956.
Note the decoration of the
rear door, simple but
entirely in keeping with
the rest of the car. Right
A Nomad of 1957*

Chevrolet

This model was chosen as the Pace Car at the Indianapolis 500. The same lines were kept for the following year's models, apart from minor modifications to the front and the rear lights. For the outlay of 2329 dollars, one could become the owner of a four-door Bel Air hardtop; air conditioning was optional. The most attractive model of the range remained the Nomad which the design department at Chevrolet considered the most perfect combination of two types of car. In 1955, 8530 Nomads were sold, 8103 the following year, and 6534 in 1957.

Determined at any price to keep up with the new designs produced by Ford and Plymouth in 1957, Chevrolet restyled the whole range. Keeping the general lines of the main part of the body, the front and rear were substantially restyled. The grille was made more open, though retaining its simplicity, while the trunk was embellished with two sharp fins. The two lights were positioned immediately below the wing, that is to say at the top of the bumpers. The engines were still the same, with the most powerful remaining at 283 cubic inches and 270 hp. With this under the hood, a Bel Air hardtop could accelerate from 0 to 60 mph in

9.9 seconds, cover a quarter of a mile in 17.5 seconds, and had a top speed of 110 mph.

In 1958 the Chevrolets were changed again. The new lines were lower, much wider, longer and especially heavier, literally as well as figuratively. In addition to the Bel Air, which maintained its relatively untroubled progress, two new models appeared: the Biscayne which, as standard, was powered by a straight six of 235 cubic inches and 145 hp, and the luxury version. This was called the Impala, and could be powered by the 283 cubic inches developing 185 hp, or by the 348 cubic-inch "big-block", which developed 280 hp. But the people who bought the Impala were not looking for pure performance. Although the big engine gave the car a top speed of 115 mph, the rest was hardly up to the same specification. The suspension was too soft, the steering was imprecise and the brakes were only strong enough. No, the Impala was really intended for the client who wanted good suspension on bad roads, plenty of space inside, and higher than average overall quality. In spite of the recession felt by all the US car industry, Chevrolet achieved sales of 1,200,000 vehicles

The Impala of 1960 remains one of the great classics with gull wings behind. Three rear lights differentiated this model from the Byscaine and the Bel Air, which each had two

The well-equipped dashboard of the Impala, with its five instrument dials. Next page *A magnificent Impala cabriolet of 1959 photographed in the greenish night light of Sweden*

that year, including 60,000 Impala. The Nomad was continued, but the two-door version disappeared to be replaced by a classic four-door brake.

Before 1959, Chevrolet had been very much the marque which had allowed the great stylistic revolutions to pass it by, so as not to alarm its own supposedly "stable" clientele, preferring to remain known for its sober, solid production. All this changed and with a vengeance. 1959 saw the introduction of an enormous car with a trunk so large that you could almost, as Tom MacCahill said, put a Piper Cub aircraft in it. The of the car was finished off with gull-wing fins, under which were positioned red rear lights of a terrifying size. The style had to be admired, if only for its individuality. The body had none of the usual sharp points and edges. Indeed, the overall impression was one of flatness; not only could you put a Piper

Cub inside the trunk, you could achieve take off on it. The grille of the 359 model was surmounted by two knife-blade openings. That year the range of Chevrolet prices ran from 2160 to 3009 dollars; it was still possible to own an Impala without going bankrupt.

The models of 1960 saw the modification of the gaping grille and the terrifying rear lights. Everything was in a much calmer vein, with the exception perhaps of the gull-wing tails divided in two. The grille now became more conventional. The whole effect represented a return to simplicity, although the cars were still more than 18 feet in length. In direct contrast to earlier engines, the Impala sports coupe could be equipped with a 335 hp engine, giving a top speed of 125 mph. Thus, Chevrolet did not entirely escape the craze for wing shapes and speed, but it never really subscribed to the fashion for more than two years.

Chevrolet

Corvair

The Corvair is in fact a Chevrolet, although this would be hard to guess unless you knew the history of the marque, especially since the company's products at the end of the Fifties were marked by their long lines. At the beginning of the Sixties the public in America began to undergo a change of consciousness. This change was marked by a much greater desire for cars which would be more economic to run. The Renaults and other small cars had begun to make their appearance in the States and there was a growing movement in the American industry for cheaper and smaller cars.

This was the first era of the "compact" car. The challenge had first been effectively taken up by Studebaker with the Lark. Then everyone else followed: Ford with the Falcon, Chrysler with the Valiant and General Motors with the Corvair.

Unfortunately, the last named soon ran into problems. After a number of tests, the lawyer Ralph Nader declared the car to be dangerous in a damning report. Its road-holding qualities were so bad that its use created the risk of an accident. The beginnings of this smaller car hardly reassured future customers. The customers, on the other hand, were very willing to be impressed by its styling and design, and by the flat-six rear engine with its characteristic noise.

What was less appreciated was the engine's lack of power. The poor little flat-six, with a capacity of 140 cubic inches, could only develop 80 hp at 4400 revs/min. This was far too little for someone who had just got out of a car with a 350 engine which could easily develop 250 hp. These were the specifications of the first model which came out in 1960 with the low-key name of 569 Sedan. Although the car had the advantage of an air-cooled engine, which avoided certain complications, the manual gearbox had only three gears. Everything about this automobile was of the poorest. The interior was sad and did not include the smallest gadget. The dashboard was dull, but the price certainly wasn't. The first model 500 cost almost

A car with the registration 63 VAIR, marking it as a Corvair of 1963. Equipped with a turbocharger, the air-cooled flat six could develop 150 hp

2000 dollars, while that of a big Chevrolet was only about the same. There was nothing about the car to promote sales: certainly not its inability to hold the road, which was caused by the excessive weight bias of the rear-mounted engine which accentuated the tendency to over-steer.

The next year, 1961, things — for which we can read sales — were to change dramatically. A four-speed manual gearbox was introduced as an option. And this innovation marked the true launching of the car. What had happened was hardly a revolution, but things did change much more violently from 1962 to 1964 when Chevrolet launched the Spyder Monza with its turbocharger.

The styling was identical but the engine now developed 150 hp. The new model was also equipped with an electrically-controlled hood and a much larger dashboard covered with instruments. The one unfortunate aspect of the new car was the price: 2800 dollars, excluding the options. This was quite enough to dampen any enthusiasm and sales never amounted to more than 40,000 models over the three years.

This car did, however, have some genuine qualities. It could accelerate from 0 to 60 mph in 22 seconds. It also had a high top speed of 112 mph, unheard of in the States for such a small car. This power did have its shortcomings. The first was the engine: top speed could not be maintained for very long nor could exciting acceleration. The engine could not stand it. Its road holding was still also very unstable, in spite of stiffer shock absorbers.

The second generation of Corvairs appeared in 1965 with redesigned bodywork. These were truly elegant cars with no superfluous chrome. The most desirable models were those which came out thereafter, which had very complete instrumentation, discreet exterior decoration, a luxurious interior. The engine had more power (140 hp) and a longer life. The flat six had been totally redesigned and was now served by

four carburettors. The turbocharged option still existed, which now developed 180 hp for 158 dollars extra. The coupe cost 2519 dollars, and the convertible 2665 dollars.

It should not be forgotten, however, that the Mustang had just been released and was having outstanding success. The Corvair was hardly able to stand up to such competition: 28,600 Corvair Corsas were made in 1965, but only 10,500 in 1966.

This agreeable little car finally reached the end of its life in 1969, without ever achieving fame. It was finally crushed by the Mustang and the new Camaro, two cars which represented the new automobile generation of the years 1965-75.

Detail of the rear lights of the 63 Corvair. In 1965, the range was completely restyled. Production was finally halted in 1969

Corvair

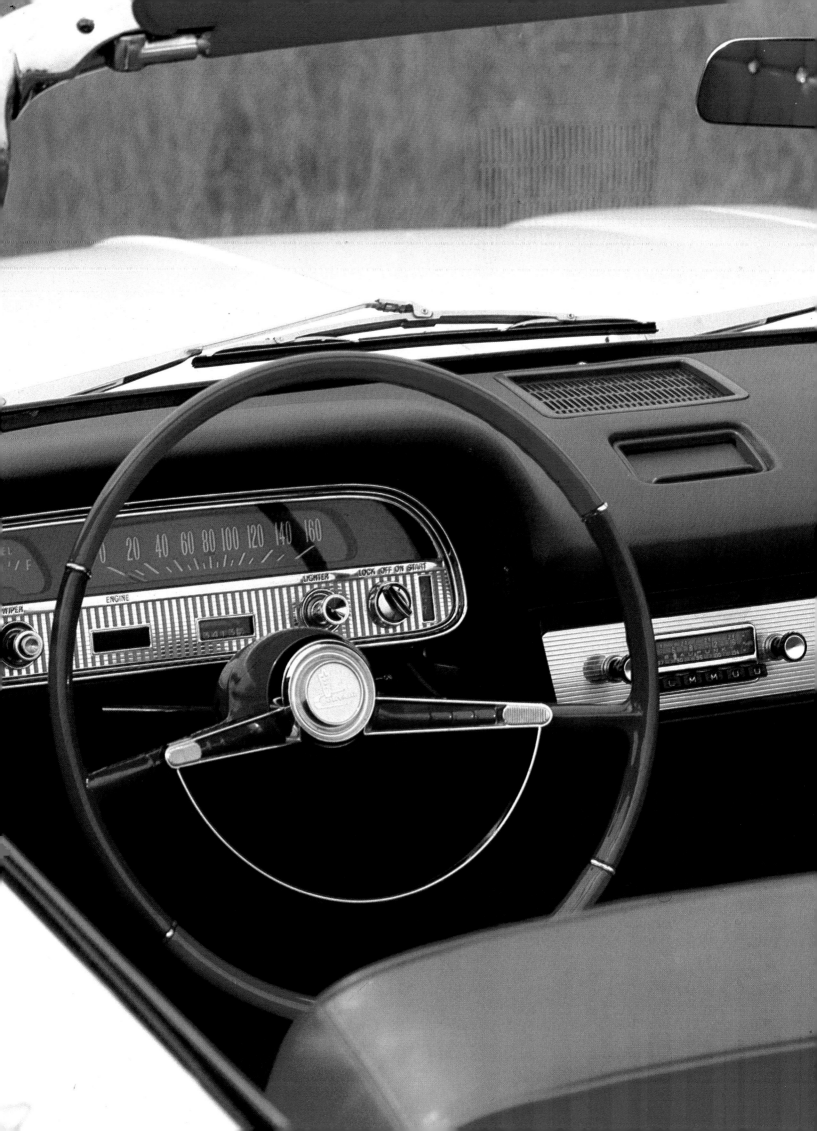

The turbo version had two large instrument panels and three smaller, while the normal 95 hp cabriolet had a much less sporty looking dashboard. The hood was not electrically operated

Corvair

Corvette

The great period of the European sports car was undoubtedly the Fifties. Three countries did battle to produce the best: England, Germany and Italy. France took almost no part in this contest of brute horsepower and pure performance.

This was also the great period of the Le Mans 24 Hours race, of the great endurance races. There were also the great rallies, such as the Coupe des Alpes and the Liege-Rome-Liege. All three countries produced an array of cars, every one as powerful as the others, but not a single American car among them.

This did not mean that the chiefs of Detroit were not interested in this market. As early as 1951, the stylist at General Motors, Harley Earl (the inventor of the fins which appeared for the first time on the Cadillacs of 1948) had given serious thought to the construction of an American sports car. Or, more precisely, a small car which would be capable of high performance and which would be specifically aimed towards the younger market. The car would have to be simple and cheap, not costing more than 850 dollars. To test the market for such a car, Earl, together with some of his staff (including the automobile design genius Ed Cole), decided to present the Corvette, a true two-seater sports car, at the Motorama Show of 1953.

The team started to work very hard on the project from May 1952; time was running short and Earl was determined to have the car ready for the show. A number of pilot designs were tried but none of them satisfied him. The project was then handed over to a certain Mr Maclean, whose method of working was quite original. Instead of starting the model of the car at the front, which was the usual practice, he started at the back.

His aim was to create an attractive looking back which, of course, houses the drive, then to position the two seats as close as possible to the drive, thus recreating one of the basic concepts of the English sports car, which had always had two seats placed well back and a huge bonnet in front. Using this principle as a starting point, he designed the first Vette prototypes, which were immediately approved by Harley Earl. The project, which was developed in the greatest secrecy, was known by the code name "Opel", nicely calculated to throw the inquisitive of the scent.

There was now no question of building the body in sheet metal for a very obvious reason. The team had now only a few months in which to complete the car's development in all aspects: body, chassis and engine. Fibreglass, which is easy and quick to work with, presented itself as an obvious alternative. Already, a short production line had been planned in the Chevrolet factory in Michigan, which would produce three cars a day.

The car was still far from being finished. The chassis and all the mechanical parts had still to be designed. The engineers had few specifications on which to base the new car, but just enough to start to resolve the problem from underneath. The idea was to make a sports car using the better components from the mass production models which would be capable of handling high performances and, above all, of making a fine driving car.

However, the chassis was an entirely new design; it was of the "ladder" type, but reinforced in the middle by an "X" to improve rigidity. The back was conventional, even a little obsolete, since it was made up of a rigid axle simply held by semi-elliptic springs, without rods or stabilisers. The front wheels were independent and lacked stabilizers. It could be said that the Chevrolet engineers were much more concerned with the simpler aspects of mechanical engineering. And in fact the engine was

the main anxiety, because Chevrolet had no unit with a high enough performance for the Corvette. It was quickly decided to modify the old straight six which had powered all the Chevrolets at the beginning of the fifties. This was the 253 cubic inches which, in its 1953 versions, developed 108 hp, or 115 hp at 3600 rpm. Ed Cole began by increasing the compression from 7.5:1 to 8:1. He then modified the inlet and exhaust systems, camshaft and a host of minor details. The most important modification was to the induction system, which was now equipped with an aluminium manifold and threee simple Carter carburettors. The old engine could now develop 150 hp at 4200 rpm. The power unit was now complete, at least for the time being. There now remained the gearbox and the decision whether to make it manual or automatic. The two-speed Power-Glide leant itself very well. In addition, it was easy to place the gear lever on the floor to give a more sporting look in inside. And so it was that the first Corvette

was produced in time for its first show in January 1953. It was looked over ant then tried by potential customers, and then came disappointment. Only 185 Corvettes were sold during the last six months of 1953 instead of the expected 300.

The failure of the car seems to have due to a number of reasons. First, there was the price. Harley Earl had originally wanted a car to sell at 1850 dollars. But the final market price was 3490 dollars. Earl had wanted to make the Corvette a young person's car, but at that price there was no question of it appealing to a youth market. Earl then changed his marketing strategy and tried to promote the car as a prestige vehicle for film stars and important public figures. This strategy also failed because the car had too rough an image. There was another important reason for the Corvette's relative failure: it's performance simply did not match up to its pretensions. Of the 10,000 planned for sale in 1954, only 4000 were built of which only 2800 were sold.

The Chevrolet Corvette of 1958 was easily recognizable by its four headlamps and the various inlets which were positioned here and there around the area of the grille. Under the hood, the usual equipment developed 230 hp. Next page The flowing rear three-quarters lacked the usual mass of chrome. However, the sales of this car were much inferior to those of the Thunderbird which became a four-seater in 1958

Corvette

1963 saw the birth of the Corvette Stingray. This was a large coupe, characterized by a two-part or split window; the following year this was modified to a one-piece

Corvette

The whole Corvette project had, then, undergone a massive loss of confidence by the end of 1954, shared by the Chevrolet management. Ed Cole, however, was still determined to pursue the project; to breathe new life into it, he recruited a Belgian of Russian origin, Zora Arkus Duntov, shortly before the appearance of the T-Bird, a direct competition. The Corvette had to find some means of surviving the success of the Ford.

In his role of experimental engineer, the first thing which Duntov did was to actually test the car properly. There were clearly a number of modifications to be made. The car oversteered; the steering was not precise enough, and the performance had to be improved. The chassis was now modified by limiting the length of the rear semi-elliptics and by incorporating a stabilizer bar at the front end, which increased the stability of the car appreciably. Duntov then planned to use a V8 engine, which had been planned at Chevrolet for several months. It was not hard to improve on the old six cylinder. Ed Cole's V8 was a small-block with 265 cubic-inch capacity, developing 195 hp. The Corvette's performance suddenly shot upwards; coupled to a three-speed manual gearbox, this engine produced acceleration of 0 to 60 mph in 9 seconds.

In spite of these important changes, which still left the styling exactly the same as before, 1955 was another critical year for the Corvette. Only 700 cars were sold, a fact which was made even more annoying by the apparently unlimited success of the Thunderbird. The Chevrolet management was not to be beaten so easily and still held strong belief in the imminent success of the little sports car.

Drastic measures were therefore used in 1956 to improve the market position of the Corvette. The first stage was to redesign the bodywork, since its original styling obviously did not appeal to the public at large. The two suppository-shaped rear lights disappeared, while the unaggressive front was replaced by a harder, virile look. The toothed grille remained, but the headlights no longer followed the bend of the fender. The sides were embellished with mouldings, although the reason for these remains obscure. The rear lights were now set in the fenders.

The new profile gave the Corvette much greater elegance — an elegance which was supposed to recall

Next page *The detailed and splendid dashboard of the 1958 Corvette. All the instruments were grouped in a single gorgeous display. In front of the driver's eyes were the speedometer, going up to 160 mph, and the rev counter. The passenger area was equipped with a solid-looking grab rail*

that of the Mercedes-Benz 300 SL. Unforunately, the first dash-board, which had been very pretty to look at but totally unfunctional, remained, although drivers consistently complained that they were quite unable to read the massive range of dials in front of them.

The six-cylinder engine and the auto gearbox were now abandoned (these had remained as options). The 265 cubic-inch V8 was retained, but much more horsepower. With a compression ratio of 9.25:1, this monster (though still small) developed 210 hp with a four barrel carburettor, and 225 hp with two four-barrels. The power of the car had now reached a respectable level, and the system was completed by a three-speed manual gearbox. It is worth nothing the performance of a Corvette specially prepared by Duntov at Daytona: a top speed of 150.583 mph. A production model could now manage 0 to 60 mph in 7.5 seconds.

Duntov was still not satisfield. He still felt the urge to do better than the European cars. The next was to try a fuel injection system, planned for two years. There were still, however, a number of teething problems with such engines. Finally, a 283 cubic-inch engine was made to yield

250 hp and 280 hp, using the special high-performance kit, which included a special Duntov camshaft Unfortunately, the kit was highly prices at 480 dollars and only 240 Corvettes thus equipped saw the light of day in 1957; the standard price was 3437. That year production of the car rose slightly to 6339 models.

In 1958, more new bodywork was designed. This was still less individual, still less "Corvette" than the preceding one. Although the rounded back was kept almost entirely, though with more wrapround bumpers, the front was restyled in a way which shocked the purists. The bumpers were made more bulky, while two phoney air intakes were placed under the headlamps. The hood was embellished with phoney louvres. The entire effect was one of contradiction of style between the rear and front ends, but this styling was to survive until 1960.

It was now the turn of the dashboard to be redesigned. The new one was a vast improvement, incorporating a very attractive instrument panel. It was still not very functional and certain dials were not visible behind the steering wheel, but the elegance of its design could not be faulted. The dashboard itself was divided in two by a console.

There were very few changes under the hood. The fuel-injection engine developed 290 hp, while another Duntov special engine developed 270 hp. The new car cost 3631 dollars, of only 119 more than the 1953 model. In 1959 and 1960 the Corvette retained more or less the same appearance. Options now became more important and a standard 1959 model, whose basic price was 3875 dollars, could cost 5000 dollars with all options.

All this did not prevent the Corvette from selling less than 10,000 models in 1959, at a time when its direct competitor, the Thunderbird, was heading towards 100,000. Would it have been better to have made it a four-seater?

Corvette

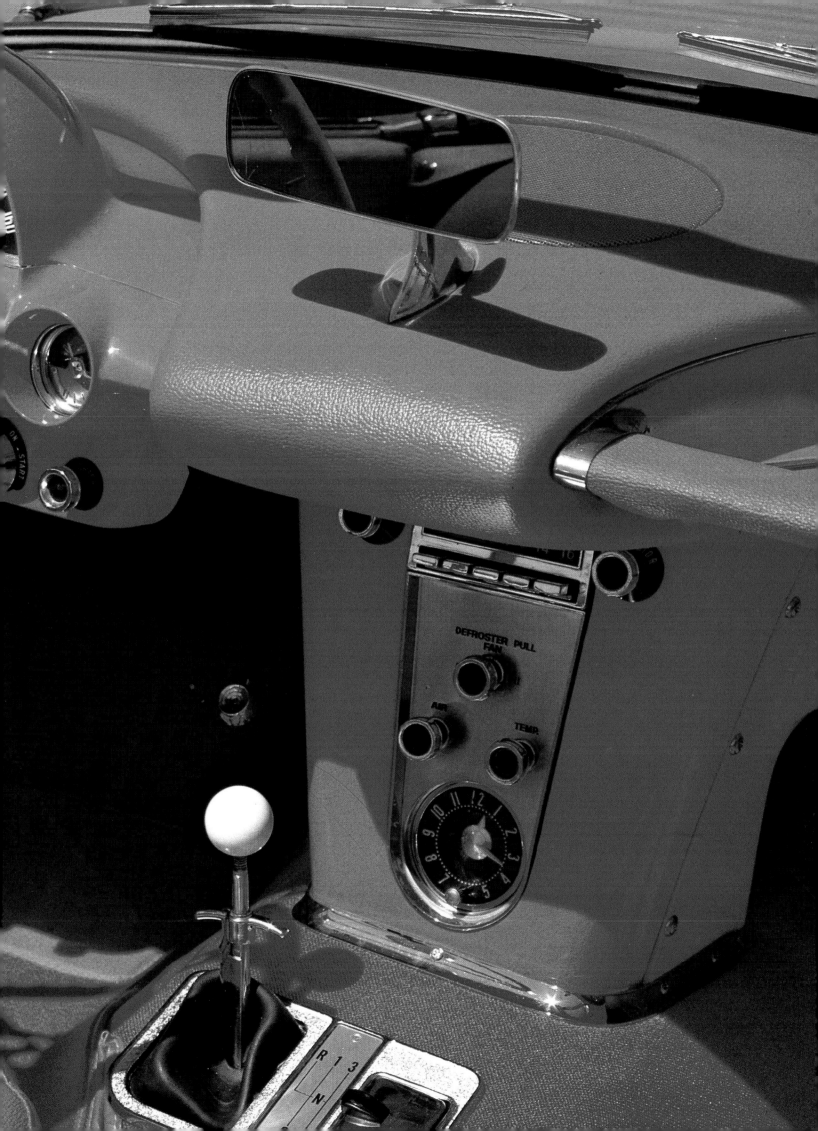

Oldsmobile

Without the presence of old Mr. Olds, there would be a gaping hole in American automobile history. His full name was Ransom Eli Olds. Long before 1900 he was already in the business of making steam engines and electrical parts, a business which finally became the Olds Motor Vehicle Co. in 1897. Olds was a man who was interested in everything that moved, and after a number of setbacks and minor successes, he produced his first car, the Oldsmobile, which was the best sold car between 1903 and 1905. The business then did less well and was bought by the famous William Crapo Durant who, together with Buick, formed General Motors in 1908.

Like a Cadillac, Oldsmobile produced a V8 in 1915. The production of this masterpiece came to an end in 1922, when all the manufacturers turned back to straight eights. Others remained convinced of the superiority of the V8 in contrast to the heavy and clumsy straight eight. How hard it is to get everyone to agree at the same time!

In 1931 there was only one model in the Oldsmobile range: the F-31, an unexciting six-cylinder car with one striking note, the Synchromesh gearbox. In 1932 Oldsmobile proudly added a straight eight to the range; equipped with an automatic choke. This was not a dramatic innovation, but it does go to prove that this feature was not invented but yesterday.

The next few years were reasonably successful, Olds hovered between fourth and ninth position in the sales league. The cars of this period were unpretentious machines, well made and of incontestable reliability. Improvements were made slowly but surely. In 1934, the Knee-Action Wheel was introduced, which gave the Oldsmobile an independent front axle. This was a very important move and one which was relected in the sales figures. Then hydraulic brakes were introduced, which cut out wheel locking, which frequently happened with cable breaks, and reduced maintenance. These improvements appeared at more or less the same time in all General Motors models, although each individual marque was still managed independently.

By 1937, however, Oldsmobile had still not introduced an auto gearbox, although something called the Automatic Safety Transmission, a sort of semi-automatic gearbox, had now been incorporated in the range. A true auto system came two years later, in 1939, in the form of the Hydra-Matic-Drive, which was offered as an option at the surprisingly low price of 77 dollars.

By the beginning of the Second World War, Oldsmobile boasted six different models in the range. These were: the Special 66-6, the Special 66-8, the Dynamic Cruiser 76-6, the same as 76-8, the Custom Cruiser 96-6, and the same as 98-8. Two things are worth noting. First, Oldsmobiles had always been designated by a number, to which was added a name. Second, the 6 or the 8 indicated, clearly, the number of cylinders.

Once again we come across Harley Earl, the GM Stylist, who had been with the company for many years. In 1948 he designed the first Olds Ponton, which incorporated two fenders in the main part of the bodywork. This was the 98, which was given the name ot Futuramic. It had softened lines, a bulging windscreen and a sulky mouth of a grille which lasted until 1955. The 98 was the top of the range; the Futuramic convertible cost 2160 dollars, compared with a standard 66-6 sedan, which sold for 1385 dollars. In spite of this gap, the sales of the Futuramic were more than 50 per cent greater than the cheaper model. It should be remembered, though, that only the 98 had been restyled and that the others still retained their pre-war shapes, with

an upright windshield and separate fenders. The drawback to the Futuramic was its engine, which was a weak side valve straight eight whose performance left a lot to be desired, although it was reliable enough.

This may seem strange, since we tend to remember the Olds as a highly competitive and powerful car. It was, indeed, in 1949 that things changed. That year the company introduced a powerful V8 which was to be the basis for everything which followed. It had overhead valves, a five bearings crankshaft, high compression... This V8 could develop 135 hp without strain. It was used in the 88 and 98, making those cars the terror of the freeways. There was no competition except for Cadillac, and then only in top speed because the Cadillacs were too heavy to accelerate fast.

The engine, called the Rocket, was also very flexible and the Olds 88 became the archetypal fast car. It could accelerate from 0 to 60 mph in 12 seconds, which was startling for the time. Top speed was 92 mph with a manual gearbox, and 100 mph with the long-case automatic transmission.

There was, however, a drawback in the models of 1951. Since the Thirties the Olds had all been equipped with coil springs on all four wheels, but they were now given very disappointing semi-elliptics at the rear. In their favour were strong stabilizer bars.

These were details, however, and there was no doubt that Oldsmobile had created a very powerful car; the 88 with the Rocket engine was devasting in stock car racing. It weighed 500 lb less than a 98, and was virtually capable of becoming airborne. Out of the nine NASCAR races of 1949, the 88 Rocket won six. In 1950 this car took the speed record for its category at Daytona, achieving an average speed of more than 100 mph. On the ovals, the car won 10 races out of 19, and the following year, 20 out of 41. It goes without saying that all this success had a marked effect on sales. Oldsmobile sold almost 400,000 cars in 1950.

Nineteen-fifty was also the year in

The instrument panel of the 1950 Olds 88. Above the semicircular speedometer were positioned the dials indicating water temperature, fuel, battery charge and oil pressure

Oldsmobile

A 1950 Oldsmobile coupe with its rounded elegant shape. The small Cadillac-style fins were already present in the form of steel protruberances. Opposite The monstrous Olds of 1958, armed like a medieval knight and carrying the "Continental Kit"

Oldsmobile

This Olds Starfire convertible was entirely redesigned in 1955. It was powered by a V8 of 185 hp

Oldsmobile

which all models were substantially restyled. The rear fenders were incorporated into the main part of the body, and the split windshield disappeared. Apart from the grille, which still had a rather sad look, the design now began to look like that of the Buicks. Prices ranged from 1719 dollars to 2772 dollars for the 98. The same year also saw the appearance of an intermediate model, the Super, with a 1195 wheelbase, like that of the 88. It was also powered by the Rocket, which could now devedop 160 hp, thanks to a quadruple carburettor mounted here for the first time on a V8 (the Quadri-Jet). The Hydra-Matic gearbox was now given an optional supplementary gear, the Super, which allowed third to be used to 75 mph. At the same time they introduced the Autronic Eye

(1953 on the Cadillacs) which made the switching from dipped to main beam and vice-versa automatic. The reason for this particular gadget was that the manufacturers had noticed that drivers never dipped their lights. The eye system was developed to try to avoid the resulting dazzle, but it did remain a subject of controversy for a number of years.

The stylistic evolution of the Olds remained slow until 1953. Any changes made tended to be minor. The 98 Fiesta did excite a lot of interest although its production was limited; the interior was covered in hand-stitched hide, while the exterior was two-toned, incorporating alpine white, red or the traditional turquoise. No options were available for this model, since it already had everything: power-assisted steering and brakes, the V8 engine, now a little old, with 303 cubic inches developing 170 hp at a compression ratio of 8.5:1, and finally, air-conditioning, although this system was rather clumsy and complex. Oldsmobile had been one of the first manufacturers to introduce air conditioning in 1941.

The year 1953 saw the end of one type of body. It was also the end of the 303 cubic-inch Rocket, which then developed 150 hp in the 88, 165 at 3600 revs. in the Super 88 and 98, and 170 in the Fiesta 98. In 1954 all the cars were restyled; there was now a grille from which sprang two "flame-throwers", a panoramic windshield and small though prominent rear lights. Especially notable was a 98 called Starfire, a very advanced model, which sold for 3249 dollars.

The 303 cubic-inch Rocket now became the 324, which developed 170 hp at 4000 rpm. in the 88. The super 88 and 98 now enjoyed 185 hp at 4000 rpm., which gave the cars very high top speeds, especially with the aid of the ratios obtainable with the long case gearbox.

In 1955, the same bodywork was retained. Nevertheless a neater, happier looking grille was introduced. This year the 88 received the 185 hp engine, while the Super and the 98 now exceeded 200 (202). The Starfire convertible continued on its prestigious way, with electric windows and seats as standard equipment; there was also an electric clock and window wiper.

The following year yet another new grille appeared, which resembled an open fishmouth. The old Rocket T350 with 324 cubic inches now developed 230 hp in the 88, thanks to a compression ratio of 9.25 and a two barrel carburettor, and 240 hp in the other two models with a four barrel carburettor.

But things were to take a turn for the worse in 1957. The new bodies were unusually strong. The hardest shape to accept was that of the Starfire 98 coupe, which now looked squat and was characterized by a three-part rear window. The grille was massive and open, a real man-eater. The J2 Rocket was especially disappointing. Oldsmobile wanted to retain its supremacy in fast, powerful cars and the 371 cubic-inch engine now developed 300 hp, thanks to three two barrel carburettors. The cars had obviously become much heavier since 1950, but they still remained very agile and could easily achieve a top speed of 125 mph and acceleration from 0 to 60 mph in 8 seconds. The lines of the Oldsmobile now began to appear rather obsolete, and the bodies were often criticised by other stylists. After all, Harley Earl was now not far from retirement. Nevertheless the sales of the Olds still maintained a very high level: around 400,000 cars a year and the fifth place in the list of manufacturers.

When we compare 1958 and 1959, it is hard to say where the madness began, but these were two years when the manufacturers held nothing back. In 1958 appeared a rear end which was so covered with chrome decoration that it was almost necessary to wear snow goggles to look at it. The back was finished off with two rear lights which looked like the rear of a jet engine in flight. The 1959 models were even more extraordinary. There were now four headlights in the grille, indicator lights in the shape of sirens, a magnificent windshield angled three ways, a Pontiac-style rear which had enough sharp edges to stop a squadron of tanks. And to send this huge heap of metal speedily on its way there was the 371 cubic-inch engine which developed 240 hp in the smaller models and a frightening 315 in the larger ones.

In 1961 this engine was replaced by the Skyrocket, with 394 cubic inches developing a maximum 325 hp at 4600 rpm. This was a welcome addition to the models of 1961 and 1962, which were notable for their sharp rears and rectangular fronts. Oldsmobile never abandoned the struggle.

Next page *A good example of an American car somewhat over restored. This Starfire of 1955 is exactly as new, and even less valuable cars are sometimes given the same treatment*

Oldsmobile

Pontiac

Pontiac is a small town to the north of Detroit. In 1907 the name was borrowed by a company, the Pontiac Buggy Company. In 1926 this was taken over by General Motors to join Chevrolet and Buick.

One of the most important events in the history of the company was the introduction of a V8 in 1924 which served the Pontiac models well until 1932. For reasons which are not very clear, this excellent V8 was then abandoned in favour of a straight eight which must have had remarkable qualities. In fact, it was only in 1955 that the management decided to develop another V8, when all other marques ware already equipped with them. It is also worth remembering that Pontiac were the first company to produce a woody station wagon, in 1937!

Until 1952, Pontiacs were recognizable by their soft, heavy shapes, the four chrome bars on the hood and the emblem of the company, representing an Indian's head, in the centre of the grille. In 1948, the Hydra-Matic gearbox was offered as an option, and the following year the Chieftain range was launched. The two-door Catalina hardtop followed in 1950. Stylistically, very little progress was made in the following years.

In fact, we have to wait until 1954 to see a redesigned back decorated with two duck's wings. This was of no great significance, but it hinted at much more exciting things to come. The dealers believed, naïvely, that the straight six and eight were at last to be replaced by a V8, since the public no longer wanted the old engines, but the year ended again in disullusionment.

All the good people, disappointed in 1954, were satisfied in 1955 when the long awaited V8 appeared. It was called the Strato Streak. It had a capacity of 287 cubic inches and developed 180 hp. The straight sixes and eights were finally obsolete. As if to do the right thing by the new unit, two series of bodies were launched: the Star Chief, with a wheelbase of 124 inches, and the Chieftain, two inches shorter. That same year a two-door station wagon appeared for the first time, like the Chevrolet Nomad.

Until 1956 the style of the Pontiac models remained rather boring; their virtue was in their large size. The sides, hood and grille seemed especially massive. The Strato Streak, however, did undergo some development; its capacity was increased to 316.6 cubic inches, developing 205 hp with a two barrel carburettor, and 227 hp with a quadruple.

And then suddenly it was 1957, when no manufacturer lost any opportunity. Everything that could be done was done at Pontiac. The fenders were tortured and cruel, while the lights were surrounded with swellings which stuck out, ending in a point behind three or four stars. The front was heavily decorated with chrome. The Star Chief had four stars ont its side, while the Chieftain and Super Chief only had three. The engines were now much more powerful, which was absolutely necessary to propel these monsters toward the synthetic horizons of the States. The Strato Streak now developed 252 or 270 hp. But the newcomer which really took the States by storm was the Bonneville convertible. This dazzlingly attractive car cost 5782 dollars and only 630 were made in 1957. It was powered by a 370 cubic-inch engine which developed 310 hp in its injection version and a little less with a carburettor. One extraordinary fact is that the version with three carburettors took 16 8/10 seconds for the quarter-mile, while the injection version needed 18 seconds for the same distance. That year, 343,000 cars were sold.

In 1958, this figure declined to 220,000, but this was much more due to the recession in the States than to the new design.

The styling was exceptionally attractive, beginning with a massive but elegant front end, including four headlamps above the heavy steel bumpers. The decoration continued down the fenders to end in two long protrusions ending just above the rear lights and the bumper. Above the trunk the extensions of the fenders divided and bore the name Bonneville in relief. The dashboard was just as dramatic, with cylindrical chromed instruments standing out from the dash. Altogether, this was a truly beautiful automobile.

In 1958, the Bonneville was chosen as the Pace Car for the Indianapolis 500. The other Pontiacs had engines varying between 240 and 255 hp. There was also the optional Air Ride, which was pneumatic suspension worked by a small 5 cubic-inch motor instead of a compressor.

In 1959, the factory making the Hydra-Matic gearboxes was burned down, and Pontiacs suddenly had to be equipped with the Powerglide or the Turboglide. Under the hood, the company offered a choice of three different V8s: The Super Strato Flash, 348 cubic inches and 280 hp, or 340 cubic inches and 250 hp, or the two versions of the Strato Flash with 283 cubic inches and 230 hp and 185 for the Mickey. But these figures are of no significance compared to the styling of the new Pontiac. The front was sober, yet threatening, almost like a sinister grin. As for the rear, no manufacturer had ever been so daring, with the possible exception of Cadillac. The bumpers were more than 15 inches high, ending at each extremity in something which looked like a submarine's ram. Above, the two warning lights looked like bread ovens. the fins were scarcely of this world and looked like two torpedoes aimed at the enemy. Those fins, in my opinion, are the most outrageous feature of any Fifties'car, which is a very considerable compliment.

A four-star Pontiac Bonneville Star Chief coupe: chrome everywhere and metal parts protruding everywhere conceivable. 1958 was a mad year for style. Next page The same excesses one year on. The stylistic violence has gone further in the lights and spurs of the bumpers

Pontiac

155

...THE OTHERS

Hudson

From 1900 to 1930 America passed through a long period of prosperity. A multitude of new companies came into existence and many of them were tempted to try their hand at automobile manufacture, thanks to the exploitation of oil. This was a great period, when car marques could be counted in dozens. But the crash of 1929 saw the disappearance of many, and from 1932 to 1940 life for the manufacturer became harder, only to become downright rough after the Second World War.

Hudson, or rather the Hudson Car Company, began in 1909. Like so many others, too, the company enjoyed a period of substantial success until the Thirties. During that period Hudson marketed a four or six-cylinder model. In 1932, the company, which had now become the Hudson-Essex, launched the Essex Terraplane, which was equipped with a 193 cubic-inch engine, developing 70 hp. Business at this time was reasonably good, but massive problems and financial losses began to make themselves felt in 1935. And, apart from a short period of prosperity from 1948 to 1952, Hudson was to remain with problems before finally going under in 1958. It is surprising, in fact, how such a company could survive so long while making losses for two out of every three years.

In 1940, Hudson had five models in its range, the most modest being the Hudson Six. Then came the Super Six, the Hudson Eight and the Country Club Eight. The losses over the range were about 2,000,000 dollars a year, but Hudson still continued.

Some success came to the company immediately after the war — the Golden Age of the Hudson. This was thanks to a superb car which had, strangely enough, been developed in 1940 by two doyens, the designer Frank Spring and the engineer Sam Frahm. Their claim to automobile genius rests on two aspects of the new car. First, because they used the monocoque construction technique on a mass-produced American car for the first time, although Nash had used the system before. For this reason, the car was called Monobilt. Second, the floor of the car was on the same level as the chassis and not above it, which made the car, launched in 1948, very low, hence the name Step-Down. The vehicle excited a lot of public interest since its low centre of gravity made it much more stable than cars constructed in the traditional manner. This was a better car than the Studebaker of 1947 with the pontoon body but with a traditional chassis.

The Hudson car, then, was something of turning point for the company. The vehicle itself was rounded in shape and had a distinctly energetic look about it. It was also the first producer of profits for Hudson for a very long time. Although the engine was the old straight six or eight, the car soon won a wide public : 150,000 were sold in the miracle year of 1948. The following year, 155000 dollars sales were achieved and the profits mounted to 10,000,000 dollars but this was not really enough to undertake a proper investment programme, in spite of the health of the Step-Down sales. Hudson then decided to introduce an

Previous page *The Hudson Hornet of 1952 with four doors and a straight eight engine, equipped with an overdrive. The little Hornet escutcheon at the front of the car lights up when the sidelights are switched on.* Below *The dashboard of the Hornet with imitation mother-of-pearl dials in plastic*

inexpensive car to the range. This was the Pacemaker, equipped with a light straight six of 221 cubic inches, developing 112 hp. The Super and the Commodore remained.

In 1951, another model was added, the Hornet 6, which was also of monococque construction. Although it was a straight six, the engine had pretensions to being modern. It had a high-compression aluminium head and, with a capacity of 308 cubic inches, developed 145 hp, which helped the car to gain a number of victories (27) in NASCAR. The following year the company produced an economy model in the Wasp series. In 1953, which was Hudson's last good year, the compactly designed Step-Down was lightened and given a small engine of 104 cubic inches. This was the Jet series which, in spite of its evocative name, made no profits. In 1954 the series was remodelled in such a disastrous way that Hudson was obliged to sign a takeover agreement with Nash-Kelvinator (refrigerators!). And from 1954 to 1958, the year when the name of Hudson finally disappeared, the decline continued.

Kaiser

On the one hand, there was Joe Frazer, first a long-standing employee at General Motors, then at Chrysler; he then worked at Willys-Overland and, at the end of 1944, at Graham-Paige. On the other, was Henry J. Kaiser, a builder of freeways, dams (Boulder Dam), bridges (Bay Bidge), tunnels and aquaducts. These two met and, in July 1945, started the Kaiser-Frazer Corporation for the manufacture of automobiles... The company bought the giant factory of Willow Run in Michigan where the assembly line was installed.

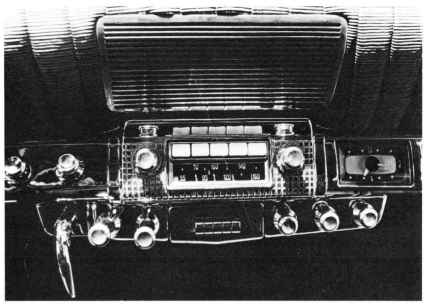

The first Kaisers appeared in 1947. These were the fourdoor-K100 Special and the K101 Custom. Hardly 5500 Customs came off the immense assembly line, although sales of 65,000 were achieved for the Special. At the same time, Frazer had remained head of the Graham-Paige Company and made his own cars, which were identical to the Kaisers but with different names. In 1947 6400 Frazer-Graham-Paiges were sold (the last of the name) and 30,000 Frazers. Although none of these sales figures is particularly startling, the two men were very capable in the business and in 1947 and 1948 they managed to sell 200,000 cars between them, although these were not of great distinction.

Without going into the complicated details of models sold in three versions and under two different names, it is worth noting that, after the K100, Kaiser did bring out a very original vehicle in 1949 and 1950: the Traveler. This was a straightforward limousine, except that it could be transformed into a brake because of the double rear door and rear seat. It was, in fact, the five-seater car of today, before its time. Then came the Virginian in sedan and four-door cabriolet versions. Although the cabriolet was undeniably a good-looking car, its lack of rigidity soon added it to the junkheap.

The great novelties of 1951 were the

The radio set of the Kaiser Dragon. Next page The Kaiser Dragon of 1953 with its very individual windshield. Below, The Darrin, with its polyester body and sliding doors. Right The Nash Airflyte of 1951 which had seats wich could be transformed into couchettes. Below An Anglo-American car, the Nash-Healey

Kaiser

idea. The styling was more modern, with such rounded lines that it was nicknamed the "elephant". The traditional grille was reduced in height and, indeed, looked very insignificant against the five-barred bumper. The shape of the car did not seem to harm sales and 90,000 of the new model were sold in 1948 and 115,000 in 1949. Apart from the increasingly powerful engines of that otherwise quiet yearn the important innovation was the Ultramatic, the only automatic gearbox ever made by an independent. It was an exceptionally fine piece of engineering too. The smoothness of the change from gear to gear was superior to that of the Cadillac's Hydra-Matic. In contrast to this excellence, though, the car was too heavy and any attempt to achieve good acceleration meant frequent gear changes. In 1949 prices ranged from 2224 to 4868 dollars. No innovations were made in 1950, and the horse power remained at 135, 150 and 160 for the heavy cars. A new range was introduced in 1951 with modern bodywork of great elegance. The standard models were called, or rather numbered, 200 and 200 De Luxe. They had a 122 inch wheelbase, while the engine was a small straight eight of 288 cubic inches, developing 135 hp. The third model was the 300, with 127 inch wheelbase, a 327 cubic inch engine developing 150 hp without strain. At the summit of the range was the Patrician 400, also mounted on a 127 wheelbase and powered by the

327 engine. To make the current engine more acceptable, it was given a crankshaft with nine bearings, overhead valves and a compression ratio of 7.8:1, to develop 155 hp. The last car of the 1951 range was the two-door 250 hardtop, which had the short wheel base but a large engine. The new lines of the Packard range, which lasted until 1953, were not especially exciting. The grille, was derived from the sumptuous works of art of previous years, which means that it was a mess of chrome. There was now a one-piece windshield, but the rest of the body had little imagination about it; in fact, it was really too ordinary and banal to grace a Packard. Until 1952, the marques emblem always affixed to the end of the hood had been a majestic cormorant, its wings pointing to the sky. Some idiot at Packard, in the supposed interests of aerodynamics, then had the wings folded back. Was this an omen of a terrible end to the company? At the time, this did not seem to be so, and the company appointed a new president (though often a bad sign) by the name of Nance in 1953. The new president was very concerned to bring some order. He wanted to increase the power of the cars and, more generally, to modernize the company. The bodywork was hardly touched and all energy was directed towards the engines. The 200 disappeared to be replaced by a Clipper (?), powered by a 288 and developing had finally lost the famous shape of

A Packard Super-8 of 1949. The decadence had started. The grille had got smaller while the bumper had started to thicken.
Next page The last Packard Caribbean, of which 275 were made in 1956. The radio had an automatic tuning system; the seat covering was reversible. Under the hood: 310 hp

Packard

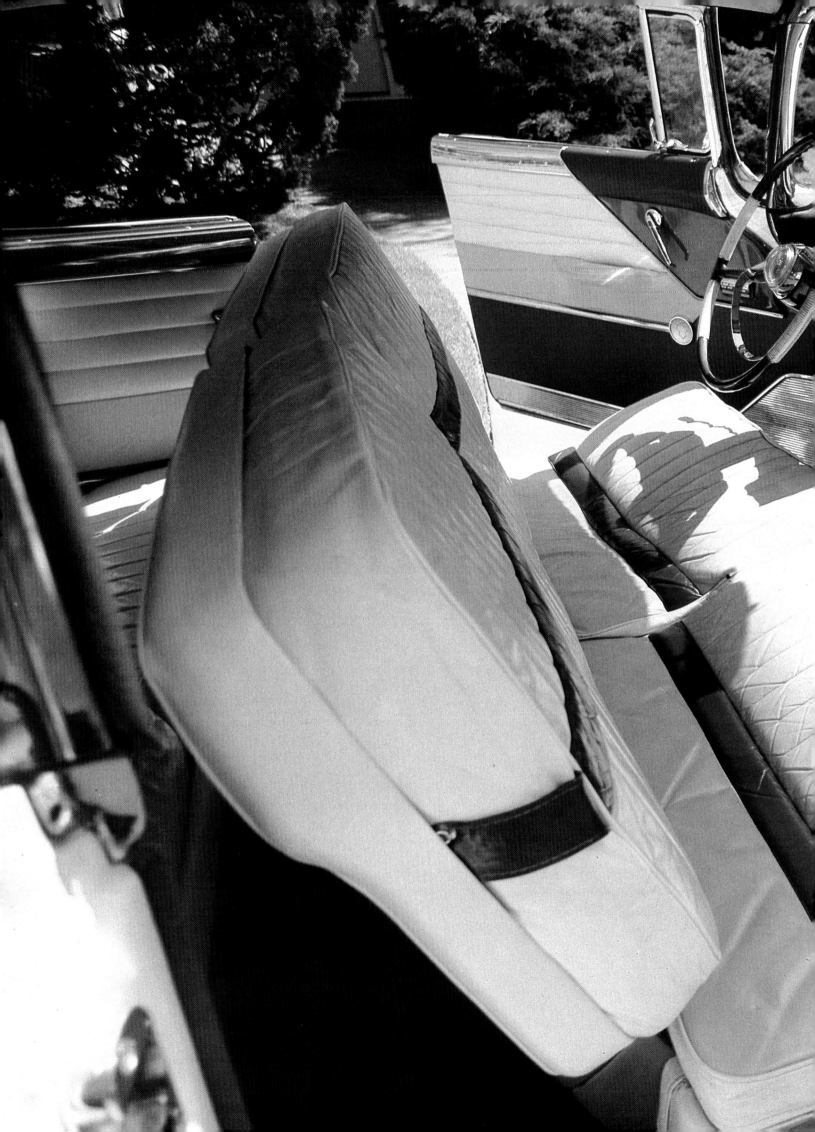

150 hp. The Clipper De Luxe with the 122 inch wheelbase received a 327 developing 160 hp. The 300 was now called the Cavalier and, right at the top of the range, the Patrician retained its old name. The range offered by Nance, then, consisted essentially of two intermediate models and two luxury ones and can be justified in commercial terms. But then Nance committed a very bad error; instead of adding two models at the low end of the range, he added yet another two luxury cars. The two-door Mayfair hardtop was powered by the huge 180 hp engine. Then came a super luxury model, the Carribbean convertible. Spoked wheels, chrome embellishment around the lower part of the body and wheels, exterior spare wheel: only 750 were sold. In spite of this, the model continued its distinguished existence until 1956, and it does remain a much sought-after car even today. But changes had already begun to happen in 1954. The first of these was the Packard-Studebaker merger.

It would be hard to say which of the two independent manufacturers was in most trouble, but after the merger the two makes retained their own models, and simply pooled their problems. The large straight eight was now improved to develop 212 hp, thanks to an aluminium head and a capacity of 359 cubic inches. This monster was intended for the final models: the Patrician, the Carribbean and the two-door Mayfair. But these changes did not yield the expected dividends and Packard sales for the year totalled only 32,000.

Nance, however, was a great optimist. He knew that a financial bedlam could not be remedied in a few months. He believed that he still had two miraculous cures for the company up his sleeve. The first involved the complete redesign of the bodies, and the second the development of a new engine.

The new bodies reflected very closely the stylistic preoccupation of the times. The lines were sweeping and streamlined. At the front, the grille the Thirties to become completely horizontal; even the thickness of the bumper was not shocking. The Clipper, with its 122 inch wheelbase in two or four door versions, survived, but the old Cavalier and its convertible version disappeared. The only cars which could still lay claim to being pure Packards were the Patrician sedan, the 400 hardtop coupe and the Caribbean.

On the mechanical side, Packard at last introduced a V8. This new development had obviously come too late; but they should be admired for having actually dared to play this last card. The new but simple engine had a capacity of 320 cubic inches, developing 225 hp. It could just about hold its own in 1955. Another innovation which should never have been introduced was the Torsion-Level Ride, which replaced the rear springs and enabled the body to remain at a constant height, no matter how heavily it was loaded. This system frequently did not work, but was standard on all three Packard models. The year of 1955, then, was full of hope for Packard. Alas, the technical improvements had come too late. The models had lost their finesse, elegance, prestige and reputation. The only way to remain alive was to raise the prices. These now ranged from 2586 dollars to 5932 dollars, the highest figure for the Caribbean, which put it in the Cadillac class.

The knell was tolled for Packard in 1956. The bodies were modified again, but appeared even uglier, with severe, pointed lines; fins and blade-sharp bumper. The torsion-Level Ride was modified and fitted to all models. All the Clippers were now equipped with the 532 cubic inch engine, developing 240 hp. The Customs had the 270 hp version. The luxury models were even more powerful: 374 cubic inches and 290 hp for the Patrician and the 400, and 310 hp to drive the generously proportioned Caribbean.

The year of 1956 was the last year of the true Packards. The name continued in existence until 1958, but only stuck on much uglier Studebaker models. A sad ending.

Packard

The body of this Caribbean has been given a three-tone treatment in cream, pistachio and maroon. The escutcheon represented an armed head on a V(8). After 1956 the Packards became Studebaker-Packards until 1958

Packard

Designed by Raymond Loewy, the Avanti was a pure marvel and has not dated. Under the hood was a 289 cubic-inch V8, which gave a maximum speed of approaching 150 mph. This car was produced by Studebaker from 1962 to 1964

Studebaker

Studebaker

Rarely mentioned now, in spite of its eccentric development, Studebaker equally enjoyed some startling successes and misfortunes. At one time or another it had successfully manufactured cars, trucks, boats, only to fail miserably in 1966 with yet another spectacular car, the Avanti.

Studebaker was a family company which went back as far as the 1850s. In 1852 the brothers Henry and Clem found themselves in South Bend, Indiana, with barely two cents between them. They did, however, manage to establish a small business in making wagons and carts. This was a good idea, since they were on the trail to the West followed by pioneers seeking fortune in Oregon or California. This traffic provided a steady stream of clients for the Studebakers and the Indian wars gave another boost to their business. By 1867 the business had an annual turnover of 350,000 dollars. The following year they started the famous Studebaker Brothers Manufacturing Co., becoming the largest producer in that part of the States of carts, buggies and horse equipment. One extraordinary fact is that it was the Studebaker brothers and not Henry Ford who invented assembly line production. In 1860 they were already capable of producing a complete vehicle in less than seven minutes: Ford only put these theories into practice in 1907.

By the beginning of this century turnover had grown to 2,500,000 dollars a year. The two brothers had already recognized that the future lay with horseless carriages and now turned to making cars. In 1902 they produced an electric car, designed by no less a person than Thomas Edison. After some disappointment with their first petrol-driven car around 1908, they succeeded in producing a car which held third place in the industry from 1912 to 1914. At the same time, they continued to make light carriages of all kinds. In 1920 they decided to devote themselves totally to petrol-driven cars. They produced a straight six engine for a car which was universally admired for its solidity.

In 1930, Studebaker had three reputable models: the President, a luxury car; the Commander; and the Dictator, a very simple vehicle. But business now began to take a turn for the worse. Only 44,000 cars were sold in 1932, which was not enough. In 1933, Studebaker was obliged to merge with White to wipe out its 15,000,000 dollars of debt. This was the first setback for what had always been a very healthy marque.

By the mid-Thirties, however, the company was on the road to recovery. A number of striking innovations were made at the time: independent front suspension, overdrive, hydraulic brakes. These were good years again for Studebaker, and 85,000 cars were sold in 1936. But the company plunged again into problems with the recession of 1938, when only 46,000 cars were sold.

The history of Studebaker was always one of constant ups and downs, where each descent almost always ended in total disaster. The bad times also seemed to have a tonic effect and the company would often start off again with renewed energy.

In 1939, therefore, the company made the conscious decision to enter the cheap car market. The gamble paid off. After four years of development, they produced the glorious Studebaker Champion (the first of the name) designed by the Raymond Loewy. Selling at 750 dollars, the new model cost just over 50 dollars more than a similar Ford or a Plymouth. But what it lost in the price war, it gained in its light weight. It was more than 500 lb lighter than its rivals, giving a 20 per cent better performance. The Champion used an engine of 164 cubic inches, developing 78 hp to give a maximum speed of 80 mph. The public was quick to recognize the superiority of the car and 106,000 sales were made in 1939. Everything was well again in the factory at South Bend.

The war came and went, and many manufacturers took up where they had left off in pre-war days.

Studebaker was the first company to produce a genuinely new car for the Fifties. This model was still called the Champion. the body, designed by Raymond Loewy and slightly modified by Virgil Exner, was revolutionary and totally modern. The pontoon body was given a strictly horizontal grille, and a one-piece windshield was introduced (in 1947!). The rear seating was in four parts — again a stylistic revolution. In contrast the engine and chassis were little changed. The fresh and unexpected design of the car ensured its success. Indeed, the success was quite extraordinary, since the Champion sold 268,000 in 1950; the majority of these were equipped with the new automatic transmission. In 1948, the Studebaker range was divided into the Champion convertible, the Sedan and a two-door, three-window version. To these was added the Commander, which had been redesigned and now cost 2,077 dollars. The 1950 model had been slightly modified, but the main part of the body remained the same. The one surprising change was in the grille which appeared to have been largely inspired by aircraft design. The nose, which only lacked a propeller, was aligned with the headlamps, while the true grille was much lower. Even at a time when aircraft design had influenced many areas of design, the grille was very unexpected. Perhaps the genius of Raymond Loewy had just slightly failed him this time, for the new car sold less well than its predecessor with the horizontal grille. The new grille was, however, retained in the models of 1951. The Commander was now equipped with an overhead valve V8 and coil springs on all four wheels.

The public does seem to have been totally prepared for the new aesthetics of the Studebaker design and the

models of 1950 and 1951 never achieved the sales of 1947-50. The best-seller was the Commander, the only one to be equipped with the V8. This engine was certainly no monster of the racing circuits, with massive power growling through its exhausts. Far from that, it was a modest 233 cubic inches, developing its 120 hp and 4000 rpm, which gave the car a top speed of 90 mph in favourable conditions. The odd shape of the car with its bullet-nose front gradually began to implant itself in the public consciousness. The Stude was gradually becoming an institution. Its price was still very modest. The standard model, the Champion De Luxe, was only 1643 dollars, while the top of the range, the Commander Land Cruiser, was still only 2289 dollars. All these factors helped make sales of more than 220,000 in 1951.

To mark the centenary of the company in 1952, the whole Studebaker range was redesigned. It would be perhaps more accurate to say that the irritating bullet-nose disappeared to be replaced a horizontal toothed grille. This was less original, but the client preferred it. A new car, the two-door Starliner hardtop, was now introduced, but sales still fell that year to 162,000, which shows that the bullet nose was not the only reason for falling sales.

The next years was one of startling change. The head of design, Robert Bourke from the Loewy studio,

In the postwar years, designers drew some of their inspiration from aircraft forms. The Studebaker of 1950 was a typical example and this front was conserved for the 1951 model. The engine was a six-cylinder. Next page The President coupe of 1955 which retained the style of the 1953 Champion

Studebaker

179

Compared with the first models of 1953, this version has been made heavier and loaded with chrome. It had a 259 cubic-inch engine which developed 175 hp

designed a very low coupé with very fine, pure lines for the year's automobile shows. After modifying a number of aspects, Raymond Loewy presented the car to the Studebaker management who agreed to put it into production. How could they have refused?

The new car was given the same wheelbase of 120.5 of the Land Cruiser and an engine of six or eight cylinders. The range included two- and four-door saloons and two types of coupe, the more streamlined of which was of striking beauty. It was low, aerodynamic and avoided all the stranger excesses of the Fifties. It was perhaps the most successful car of that decade. But in spite of its beauty, finesse and all its other qualities, the public remained hesitant and only 186,000 cars were made in 1953. There were few changes in 1954 and the range remained more or less identical to that of the previous year. But sales now fell dangerously low to 85,000. Clearly the unit cost of manufacture for an independent like Studebaker was much greater than for the huge groups. The engines lacked power, especially the 101 hp six-cylinder which was already obsolete in 1955. The V8 of that year

were thankfully given a little more muscle. The V8 used in the Commander had a capacity of 224 cubic inches and developed 140 hp. The President was equipped with a 259 cubic inches developing 175 hp, as was the top model of the range, the President Speedster hardtop, whose claim to distinction resided in its two-tone colour scheme and its brushed aluminium dashboard. But the price was too high at 3200 dollars. In 1955, Studebaker sold only 112,000 cars, when it was necessary to sell 250,000 not to lose money.

As we saw above, Studebaker had already merged with Packard in 1954. The merger was not especially beneficial to Packard, which lost its own models in 1956, to be replaced by the Studebakers modified in front and behind which then carried the name of Packard for two years.

The production of Studebakers did, however, continue in 1956, but the financial position of the company remained critical. The new lines were heavy and uninspired. A cheap two-door model, the Sedanet, was introduced, as well as the Hawk coupe series. The Hawks were bastardized versions of the attractive 1953 coupe, conserving the passenger compart-

Studebaker

ment. The front and back, however, were modified with a chromed grille and small fins. The range stretched from the Skyhawk to the Golden Hawk by way of the Flight and Power Hawk. Studebaker had thus placed a lot of hope in its coupe range, which was powered either by a six-cylinder engine or by various V8s of which the most powerful developed 275 hp. As time went on, these cars seemed less and less attractive. After the disappearance of the Studebaker-Packards in 1958, Studebaker continued its production entirely on the Hawk series. The front and back were remodelled every year until 1962, the year in which the car was totally redesigned to create one coupe, the Hawk GT, which then sold for 3,424 dollars. During the same period, the company had also entered the small car market with the Lark, introduced in 1959. This was a thick-set car, powered by a six-cylinder or V8 engine. The top of the range was the Lark Daytona propelled by a V8 of 225 hp. The Last of the Larks was produced in 1963.

What, then, remained for this famous rame after the death of the Lark and a hundred years of distinguished manufacture. Only the Hawk GT and a newcomer, the last chance, the Avanti. This beautifully designed car, with its outstandingly attractive front end was once again the work of Raymond Loewy. It was a two-door coupe with a polyester body which had the remarkable feature of having no apparent radiator grille. As in the case of the Citroen DS the air intake engine cooling was positioned beneath the bumper. The new chassis built by Studebaker for this car had a wheelbase of 109 inches. The Avanti was propelled by a small V8 of 289 cubic inches developing more than 200 hp. But there were other engine options. The gearbox was a Borg-Warner automatic; the front wheels were equipped with disc brakes. The price of the Avanti was 4759 dollars, but the production of this marvellous car came to an end on 9 December 1964; only a small number of unsold models could be found on the market after that date.

The company continued to produce a number of more or less odd models, with names like Wagonaire, Commander, Daytona or Cruiser, in small quantities, before the factory in South Bend finally closed its doors in March 1966.

The President was the top of the Studebaker range and was recognizable by its two-tone colour scheme and its brushed aluminium dashboard

Studebaker

Tucker

The Tucker company is full of ambiguity. Was it crooked or simply brilliant? Was it run on entirely fraudulent lines or did it merely practice flexible accountancy? The truth now lies in its purest form in the grave of Preston Tucker, an exile in Brazil until his death in 1956.

This is perhaps the most interesting story of the postwar automobile industry. The cars themselves cannot be strictly called "Fifties" cars, since they were built between 1946 and 1949, but many of the solutions applied to their manufacture by the brilliant Tucker were very much of the following decade.

The founder of the company was called Preston Tucker. He was known to have been born in 1903, and that he hade exercised various professions, including those of cop and car salesman. He then became an engineer, and during the Fifties he went to reside at Ypsilanti in Michigan.

His aim was simple: to construct and produce the most revolutionary car ever. About 1946 he rented an old factory in Chicago which had been occupied by Dodge Aircraft during the war. The prototype of the car was produced there; this was rather derisively referred to as the "Torpedo".

The first problem to be attended to in detail was the body. The design was the work of Alex Tremulis who had in the past worked for Auburn, Cord and Duesenberg. There was no doubt, then, about his talent as a designer. The four-door saloon was very much in the "fastback" style, with the rear falling away. The body was a pontoon type, with the bulbous bumper adding an interesting and elegant design feature. The four doors were taken up into the roof to facilitate entry to the interior. The windshield was only in two parts because it was then quite impossible to find one which would hold as a single unit over such a large area. In front there were three headlamps, the centre one of which turned as the front wheels were turned. For this reason the Tucker was nicknamed the Cyclops. The front bumpers included grille with air intakes, which allowed the interior to be well ventilated. Behind, the same grille design was repeated, but this time for the cooling of the engine, which was boosted by the air intakes located in the front part of the rear fenders.

The engine was a monster of 589 cubic inches, but developed a modest 150 hp; it was originally a flat six, crankshaft with four bearings, overhead valves and with fuel injection. This engine never worked well and six engines were finally made, of which one was chosen for the Tucker. The final version was an air cooled flat six of 335 cubic inches, developing 166 hp. It was made entirely in light alloy and weighed 320 lb. The claims, unverified, for this car's performance were considerable: 0-60 mph in 10 seconds and 0-100 mph in 33 seconds; top speed of 120 mph. The engine was placed in the rear for good traction. Four wheels independent suspension was necessary.

Any resemblance found between this car and those of the present day would be perfectly justified. The design was a very long way from the

Previous page *A superb Tucker posing with the Golden Gate bridge in the background; a very advanced car for its time. The central headlamp pivoted with the front wheels and gave the car its nickname of the "Cyclops". Below One of the last water-cooled engines, although the six cylinders were originally air-cooled*

sumptuous confections of the time, its engine would not disgrace a present-day high-performance car, the centre of gravity was lower than the wheel axles and the interior was also finished very carefully. In fact, this car was so revolutionary that no one could take it seriously.

Preston Tucker found it impossible to sell such a machine at the standard price of 2485 dollars which eventually rose to 4235 dollars; even at this price the car was still sold at a loss. The interior was full of ultra-modern gadgets. The dashboard had been designed with passenger security in mind: all the instrumentation was positioned beneath the steering wheel. In a collision the front seat passengers were protected by a high-security cell. The glove compartments were incorporated in the doors.

It would be hard to visualize such a car being designed again, and this was in 1946. There two questions to be asked about the whole operation: was this really the dream car it purported to be, or was the whole operation just a vast confidence trick, since Preston Tucker had borrowed 25,000,000 dollars from dealers to finance the production? There remains the mystery as to how these funds were used, because Tucker also sold shares in the company so that the car could finally be put into production. In the event, the vehicle was never brought into production, nor its development finished so that it could take the road in complete security. Tucker eventually managed to construct 51 vehicles all which were improperly finished to a greater or lesser degree.

Almost inevitably, then, a government inquiry into a possible fraud was started. A number of Tuckers associates disappeared immediately, though Tucker and seven others did appear before the tribunal of inquiry.

The findings of the tribunal on the esential point of the use of the 25,000,000 dollars remained nebulous and everyone was acquitted. The mystery remained along with the 51 cars.

In 1950, in spite of his setbacks, Tucker commissioned Alex Tremulis to design another superb aerodynamic car with the seductive name of Talisman. The project never had a future and Preston Tucker finally emigrated to Brazil with plans to launch a small economy car. He died there in 1956. All the mysteries remain.

The Tucker was styled as a "fastback", but with four doors. The rear grille echoed the design of that in front

Tucker

*We wish to express our deepest thanks to all those who have helped us to complete this book, especially the many collectors in the United States who have not hesitated to lend us their cars for the photographic sessions and to dedicate a considerable amount of their own time to listening to us and answering our questions. Special thanks is due to Mr Gene Babow, who helped us to find the finest cars in the San Francisco region, and to Patrick van der Stricht, whose knowledge of American cars is unsurpassed in Europe.
Our final thanks are due to the American Tourist Office and to Mrs. Leonor Frye for having helped us in our task and guided our researches.*

All the photographs in this book are the work of Alberto Martinez, with the exception of those on: pages 132-133 and 149 (Anders Albinsson), pages 142-143 (Jacky Morel) and page 97 (William Borel).

ACHEVÉ D'IMPRIMER
SUR LES PRESSES DE BERGER-LEVRAULT
A NANCY EN JUILLET 1986
DÉPÔT LÉGAL : AOÛT 1986 — 778039-7-1986
IMPRIMÉ EN FRANCE